BLUE MOUNTAIN MEMORIES

*A Story of a Blue Ridge Mountain
and the People who live there*

By Richard Long

Richard F. Long

Bloomington, IN   authorHOUSE®   Milton Keynes, UK

AuthorHouse™
1663 Liberty Drive, Suite 200
Bloomington, IN 47403
www.authorhouse.com
Phone: 1-800-839-8640

AuthorHouse™ UK Ltd.
500 Avebury Boulevard
Central Milton Keynes, MK9 2BE
www.authorhouse.co.uk
Phone: 08001974150

First published by AuthorHouse 10/13/2006

ISBN: 1-4259-6778-7 (sc)

Library of Congress Control Number: 2006908648

Printed in the United States of America
Bloomington, Indiana

This book is printed on acid-free paper.

BY THE AUTHOR

History of Le Moyne College- 1951

"Nowhere A Stranger"
Story of the Medical Mission Sisters—1968

"Blue Mountain Memories" 2006

PLAYS

"Shenandoah Night Train" – 1978

"A Private Matter" – 1978

TV MOVIE

"Shenandoah Night Train" – The Movie – 1982
(Winner of an Ace - top award of Cable TV- 1983)

DEDICATED TO

Vi Baluyut
We Walked the Happy Trails of Blue Mountain Together

And to

Henry and Colette De Longfief
Their vision created the unique Place that is Blue Mountain

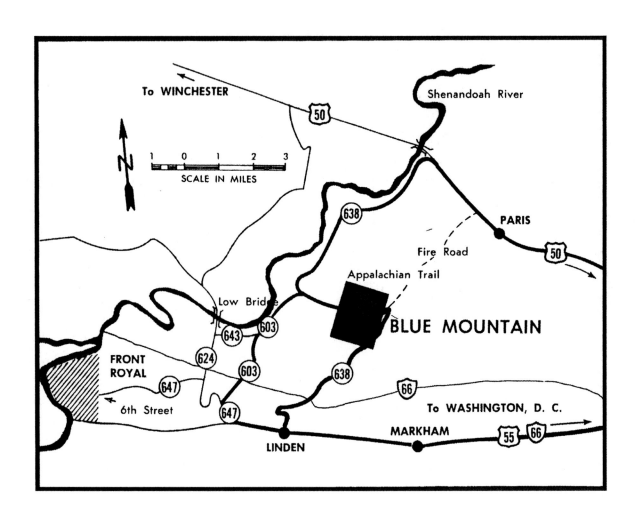

PREFACE

I remember walking along a Blue Mountain road in 1970 and coming upon one of the residents kicking a tree. All I could hear was:

"Damn that Henry--- Damn that Henry!"

The resident had been coming to the Mountain since the early 60s. I was a recent arrival. And like many newcomers I had been captured by the exuberant charm of a man who was known by many names: "Henry" "The Frenchman" "That man" and other names that will not be printed here.

The man kicking the tree was directing his anger at Henry de Longfief, the founder and builder of Blue Mountain. Henry would not let him put a swimming pool on his property.

Years later, several years after Henry died, I heard the same man stand up in a meeting of property owners at Blue Mountain and decry what he considered was a violation of the Blue Mountain covenants.

"Well," he said, with finality, "That's not the way Henry would have wanted it."

So much for consistency.

This book is not about Henry de Longfief. But Blue Mountain is very much about Henry de Longfief. Blue Mountain is still a beautiful, quiet retreat from the world because of the vision of this vibrant, mercurial Frenchman and his wife Colette.

All the time I was writing this book I felt Henry's persence. This is a roundabout way of thanking him and Colette for their cooperation in helping me in the preparation of this book.

Several other people helped me in the preparation and research for this book. To all of them I express my deepest thanks. They are:

Jack Davis and the Blue Mountain History Committee he started including: Anne Anderson, Cathy Berger, Rob Fishman, Eric and Helga Heiberg, Bill Jahn, Missy and Jim McManaway, Jason Miller, Cathy Price, Don Richards, Norm and Marcia Smith.

A special thanks to two marvelous friends: Connie Pena and Sharon St. Amand of Front Royal; my late, beloved brother Father Robert Long; my sister, Margaret Long, always a wonderful support; Jan Du Plain, Joan Marcoccia, Art Purvis, Cornell Stoots, Esta and Harlan Westover.

A special thanks to my good friend and excellent photographer Donald Mankin. Right from the beginning thirty years ago, Donald was with me on most of my more than 60 interviews I conducted for the book. His marvelous photographs add significantly to the quality of the book. The most important contribution to this work is Vi Baluyut, the love of my life for the past forty years. We found Blue Mountain together 35 years ago. It added great joy to both of our lives.

Richard Long, Auburn, NY 2006

Contents

PREFACE IX

~1~ HOW IT ALL BEGAN 1

~2~ CHARLIE REYNOLDS – THE MOUNTAIN MAN 5

~3~ FINDING A "PLACE" AGAIN 13

~4~ AU REVOIR HENRY DE LONGFIEF 17

~5~ BLUE MOUNTAIN—CLOSE TO AMERICAN HISTORY 23

~6~ LUMBERING AT BLUE MOUNTAIN, OR-OLD MCDONALD HAD A FARM . . 27

~7~ THE MARTINS ~ BLUE MOUNTAIN CIRCA 1958 33

~8~ A LINK WITH THE CIVIL WAR 37

~9~ AGNES MCDONALD –BIRDS AND A BEAR 45

~10~ FREEZELAND – THE GREAT ORCHARD 51

~11~ 1906 – THE FIRST SUMMER VISITORS 57

~12~ CHILDHOOD MEMORIES –
RIDING A PONY ON BLUE MOUNTAIN – CIRCA 1930 65

~13~ LARRY LEHEW: WELL-DRILLING, GEOLOGY, AND AN ANTE-BELLUM
SOUTHERN MANSION 71

~13~A ~ LEHEW FAMILY HISTORY 83

~14~ THE WHITES: LINDEN, WHEN IT WAS A BUSTLING TOWN 87

~15~ SOLDIERS, MONKS AND THE SHENANDOAH 93

~16~ THE CLARKS FROM ALL OVER THE WORLD TO BLUE MOUNTAIN 99

~17~ ON THE TRAIL WITH LEE LIPSCOMB 103

~18~ MOSBY'S RANGERS AND BLUE MOUNTAIN 109

~19~ THE ROAD TO LITTLE AFRICA 119

~20~ THE WESTOVERS ~ ENDING UP WHERE IT ALL BEGAN 129

EPILOGUE 135

BIBLIOGRAPHY FOR "BLUE MOUNTAIN MEMORIES" 137

BLUE MOUNTAIN MEMORIES

By Richard Long

- 1 -
HOW IT ALL BEGAN

My romance with the Shenandoah Valley of Virginia began more than fifty years ago. Shortly after I graduated from an Upstate New York college in 1951, a college friend, Carl Roesch and I, promised ourselves one last fling before we faced the world of work. We decided to visit three states we'd never seen; Kentucky, West Virginia and Virginia. All three had their charms but we both agreed the highlight of the trip was the day we came into the Shenandoah Valley from West Virginia and visited the small college town of Lexington, Virginia. Lexington, we were to learn, is a Civil War citadel of the Old South. After the war General Robert E. Lee spent his last years as the president of what was then Washington College. After his death, in his honor, it became Washington and Lee.

The revered Thomas Stonewall Jackson taught military subjects at Lexington's Virginia Military Institute. The mortal remains of both Lee and Jackson are at rest in Lexington. The white and red Georgian mansions of Washington and Lee and the haunting summertime stillness of the old parade ground at VMI have been indelibly etched in my mind since that day. On returning home, I spent the rest of the month completing Margaret Mitchell's voluminous "Gone With the Wind."

It would be fourteen years later, after a wide-ranging career as a newspaperman, that I would return to this area as a Washington correspondent for New York State newspapers. The story of how I came to build a summer home at Blue Mountain, Virginia and got to know the people of the Blue Ridge, is the subject of this book.

This book has started several years ago in the 1970s during a year-long sabbatical from my work. It was put aside, unfinished, when I received an opportunity for a career producing television documentaries.

An interesting set of circumstances re-stimulated my interest in finishing this book. When I did the original research for the book in the 1970s I was pleasantly occupied by my love and respect for the Virginia people I met, by the beauty of their state and by its all-encompassing history from Colonial times to the present.

"The whole history of America is in that state," a friend reminded me.

During my research I found myself envious of the people who were rooted here, who were part of the fabric of this area. Although I am proud of my Upstate New York heritage it is part of my split personality to have a deep fondness for Virginia, too. I am a Yankee who loves the South.

A curious, serendipitous experience happened to me while I was browsing in the Pentagon book store several years ago. Tucked away, amongst the books on the Civil War was a new book. The title was: <u>Ruggles' Regiment—The 122nd New York Volunteers in the American Civil War</u> by David B. Swinfen (University Press of New England). I picked it up hesitatingly. Upstate New Yorkers are always, it seems, overshadowed by their big city to the south. I thought the book would be about a New York City regiment.

Surprisingly, it was not. Not only was it about an upstate New York regiment it was about a regiment from Syracuse, my hometown, and Onondaga County. I didn't know of any family members who were in the Civil War. But I remember going quickly to the back of the book where the names of individual soldiers were listed alphabetically. There it was; as sharply remembered now as anything I have ever read: "Long, Patrick—21 (age)- 23 March 1864 (date of enlistment)—D (company)—Pte. (rank) – 23 June 1865 (date of discharge)."

I was startled. I had never heard of any member of our family being in the Civil War. Skepticism overtook me. There were a lot of "Longs" in Syracuse and Onondaga County, I thought. I started to read the book. The regiment, the author wrote, was composed of Syracuse lawyers (the officers) and Onondaga County farmers (the enlisted men). Hmmm! My ancestors were Irish farmers who came to Onondaga County from Ireland in the 1850s and settled in the towns of Pompey and Fabius.

Luckily, my nephew, Stephen Long, had done some family research several years before my discovery of the Ruggles book.

He sent me a copy of his research. I looked up my own file on family history. Startled again. Stephen's research showed that there *was* a Patrick Long in our family. He would have been the brother of my grandfather, or my great uncle. To make it even better he was born in 1844 which matched the date, 1864 and the year (21) when he enlisted.

Again I put the information aside. What brought it to light even more recently was a trip out to the Shenandoah Valley for a Civil War re-creation of the significant battle of Cedar Creek which took place on Oct. 19,1864. Cedar Creek was important because it was the last stand of the Confederacy in the Shenandoah Valley. The battle involved more than 50,000 troops on both sides and when it was all over there were about 7,000 casualties. Such famous generals as Philip Sheridan and George Custer were on the Union side and General Jubal Early commanded the Confederate forces.

What I found most interesting however was the makeup of the various units. The famous Union VI Corps participated and its Second Division, I learned, contained the 122nd New York Infantry, Uncle Patrick Long's regiment. General Early's astute maneuvering on the morning of the battle caused several Union units to retreat. The exception, for some time, was the Second Division of the VI Corps, which held the Union line. Early, in his later recollection of the battle said he thought he was fighting the whole VI Corps, only to realize it was mainly the Second Division. The Confederacy won the morning battles, but, in the afternoon Sheridan rallied his forces and through his victory gained military control of the Valley.

Uncle Patrick's regiment returned to the battle at Petersburg and Richmond. When the war ended. the regiment history reports, they were in the vicinity of Appomatox where General Lee surrendered to General Ulysses S. Grant.

Earlier, I mentioned that I was envious of people who had their roots in the Valley. After researching the role of my great uncle I realized that, although it was a tragic event, certainly for the South, the battle of Cedar Creek had more significance for me because he was present there. There is a point on top of Blue Mountain, in front of the Community Lodge (which used to be the restaurant) where, on a clear day you can see forty miles to the Alleghenies in West Virginia. From that point, too, in October of 1864, the smoke from the gunfire and artillery fire of the Cedar Creek battle would have been clearly visible.

I often think of my Uncle Patrick when I look out over the Valley from that point. He is my "connection" to the past and the present.

Several years ago when I finished some of the chapters of the book I gave them to a friend to read. Her reaction was: "You really like that old black man, Charlie Reynolds, don't you?" I admitted that I did like Charlie, who was then approaching 90 years. I used to spend a lot of time on the front porch of his old farmhouse. The chickens and the cats would run around in the yard while Charlie told me about the old days on the mountain.

My friend suggested that it would be a good idea if I talked to Charlie again to "dig out some more stories." I agreed that it was a good suggestion. I called Charlie a few days later to set up another appointment . To my shock I was told that Charlie (who had been in ill health) had suffered another stroke. I rushed out to the Warren County Hospital in Front Royal to visit him. Sadly he was in a delirious state and could not carry on a conversation. Charlie died a few days later.

I think it fitting that I begin the book with the chapter I had finished on Charlie before his death.

- 2 -
CHARLIE REYNOLDS –
THE MOUNTAIN MAN

The roads to Blue Mountain history begin at Charlie Reynolds' doorstep.

Fifty years before Blue Mountain received its name, Charlie was helping his father build rock fences.

"I was born in an old house across the woods here," the elderly black man said as he pointed across the field toward the forest. He was born December 4, 1894.

"I was brought here when I was two years old. See up there. I remember when that was growed up in pine trees. My daddy cut all of that off to build this part of the house with logs."

Although the Reynolds house is stucco finish on the outside, the interior is made of logs. It was built in the 1890's.

John Reynolds, Charlie's father, was born "sometime after the Civil War" in nearby Rappahannock County. His mother, who died when Charlie was "four or five years old" was a native of Warren County.

"I remember, I was just a little fellah. I sat on one side of the coffin and my sister sat on the other," he said.

Charlie's parents were not slaves, he said, but he did have an uncle and a great aunt who were born slaves and lived near Blue Mountain during the time of the Civil War and before.

"My uncle Jim was a slave and his mother was a slave. As a boy I used to set around and listen to my uncle talk about the Civil War. There was fightin' all through here, he told me, and lotsa' times people used the mountains to hide in when the Yankees come," Charlie recalled.

Charlie, who is in his 80s, hasn't been feeling too well the past several years. His left arm is paralyzed as the result of two strokes. But he loves to sit on his porch, surrounded by his chickens, facing the old red barn he helped his father build 70 years ago and talk about the "old days."

When I was first inquiring about the history of the mountain I was having a conversation with Mrs. Marge Martin, who with her late husband, Everett, built the first house on the "new" Blue Mountain.

"Well," she said, "I think you better start with Charlie Reynolds, he knows more than anybody else. He helped us build our house."

Charlie's memory goes back not only to the days of lumberman Jim Mcdonald, but also to McDonald's father, Sam.

"Why I knew old Sam McDonald," Charlie said. "He had a mill. When I was a youngster I would take corn to his mill to be ground up. It was operated with an old steam boiler. They pulled it with horses and set it up, wherever they found water, usually along the Shenandoah river," he said.

Charlie's house is also a landmark in the area. Like most mountain areas it is difficult to give precise directions.

You'll hear many conversations that go like this:

"It's the third house below Charlie Reynolds place, on the left."

Or

"It's up this way, just above Charlie Reynolds house."

Charlie's 30 acre farm is off route 638 about midway between the little village of Howellsville and the Blue Mountain information office. He lives there with his second wife, Mrs. Lena Reynolds, and his faithful friend and helper, Phillip Williams. Charlie's first wife died in 1968. They had seven children. All of the Reynolds children have left the old homestead and live with their own families in the Washington metropolitan area. They make regular visits to their father, usually on weekends.

The present Mrs. Reynolds was born on July 4, 1894, near Orleans, in Fauquier County. As a child, Mrs. Reynolds educated herself, taking lessons by mail.

"By the age of nineteen, I had the equivalent of a high school education," she said. She went to New York City as a young woman "and got a job sewing in a factory," But in later years her love for the South and her old friends called her back. She returned to Virginia in 1940. She got a job as a nurse on an estate for an old Virginia family nearby.

"I remember when the old Colonel died his wife said to me, 'Lena, I want you to stay, because we love you.' Well, I stayed with them for twenty-three years. Then I met this young man," she said with a smile as she pointed to Charlie.

Phillip Williams, who is also a well-loved figure in the Blue Mountain area, came to live with Charlie's family "when I was nine years old," he said. He is in his 70s now.

Charlie Reynolds held the contract to pick up trash weekly at Blue Mountain and other nearby developments. Charlie and Phillip, for years, were a familiar sight on the Mountain, making their rounds on Monday morning in the trash truck.

Making the trash run put Charlie in weekly contact with practically everyone at Blue Mountain.

"I know everyone on that mountain," Charlie says, with a strong tone of pride in his voice."

"He really does," Mrs. Reynolds says. "And a lot of them stop by to visit from time to time, especially the ones that have lived up there for awhile."

But Charlie's roots go much deeper than the 20-year history of Blue Mountain.

Sam McDonald. Heatherington. Captain Lehew. Jim McDonald. Loy Rosenberry. Henry de Longfief.

Those names are all intertwined with the history of the Blue Mountain. They span a time period of 140 years. Charlie Reynolds knew them all.

Several years before Jim McDonald took his family to live in the house (near the lake parking lot) a family by the name of Heatherington lived there.

"I remember," Charlie said, "a man used to live there that handled bees. He had bee hives. Yes, that was before Jim McDonald bought the place. I think this man's name was Heatherington.

"I was just a boy. So it must have been around nineteen hundred or shortly after.

"I never will forget it. You know how people is. They real nice people. They sent us out a pie. And we didn't like the pie. It was what you call a mince meat pie. And we wondered what are we going to do. We didn't want them to know. So we dug a hole and buried the pie."

Charlie has a boyhood friend Loy Rosenberry, who was born in Howellsville in 1902. Ronsenberry, who is retired now, and lives in Front Royal, remembers that his "great grandfather Bill Rosenberry operated a distillery at Blue Mountain" right near the site of the present de Longfief home.

Rosenberry cannot remember the exact dates.

"But it was before I was born, so it must have been in the eighteen-nineties," he said. He remembers his family talking about it.

It was a legal distillery, Rosenberry said, because it was "before the days of prohibition." Another legal distillery, Brandy Camp, was located a short distance from the Howellsville Methodist Church.

Rosenberry said that the Blue Mountain distillery was called Shiny Rock. They made apple jack and peach brandy, using apples and peaches grown nearby.

"Bill Rosenberry lived in a house right there close to where Henry de Longfief was buried," Rosenberry said. The de Longfief burial site is a short distance from the de Longfief home.

"In those days it used to be called the Lehew place. Captain Lehew owned it and he used to run his sheep and cattle up there. He lived across the river (The Shenandoah). He used to bring them over in the Spring every year and let them graze," Rosenberry said (Capt. Francis Wesley

Lehew was a Confederate officer in the Civil War. His connection with Blue Mountain is the subject of another chapter in his book).

Rosenberry said his great grandfather operated the small Shiny Rock distillery with another man, Bill Watkins.

Loy Rosenberry remembers a happy childhood in the Blue Mountain area, highlighted by summertime swims in the nearby Shenandoah River.

"Lord have mercy, me and Charlie and his brother Leonard, we had fun" Rosenberry recalled. (Leonard Reynolds, Charlie's younger brother, died of tuberculosis when he was 21 years old. Charlie thinks the year was 1914.)

"We would steal off to the river and go swimming, all three of us," he said.

In later years Rosenberry's talents as an auto mechanic proved invaluable in the remote mountain area.

"Charlie had one of the first Model T cars in this area and I used to work on it all the time," he said.

He also remembers the first time they saw one of the "horseless carriages" come to the area. He thinks it was about 1914.

"There we were one day up on this hill," he said. "We hear this rattlin', we didn't know what it was. We ran out on the road to see it and here was this car."

Rosenberry got on of the first cars in the area.

"Then Frank Oliver got one. Charlie Reynolds got one. Hedrick Jackson got one. Willie Barber got one. Chapman got one. All Model Ts."

Rosenberry's interest in automobiles, which he learned from his father, John Rosenberry, led to the founding of his own garage at Main and Water Streets in Front Royal. He operated the garage from 1938 to 1968.

Rosenberry's roots also go back to the early lumbering days in the valley and the mountains. His family originally came from Pennsylvania. His grandfather, Ash Rosenberry, owned a sawmill in Fort Valley that was operated by his father, John Rosenberry.

"After my grandfather sold his sawmill my father worked for Jim McDonald," Rosenberry said.

Loy Rosenberry was born in Howellsville across the road from the house where the McDonald's lived in 1925 after they left their Blue Mountain home. The Rosenberry house burned in a fire in 1930.

Charlie Reynolds said that after Mr. Heatherington left he remembers several people renting the old houses up on Blue Mountain.

"Then old man James Mac came along and he bought all that side of the mountain," Charlie said.

"He was a great man, James McDonald. I knowed his father. I knowed all his sisters. He didn't have no brothers. There was just one boy and a big bunch of girls."

Charlie's link with the Civil War is mostly through the recollections of his uncle Travis.

"My uncle Travis had a brother Jim who was a slave. And Uncle Travis' mother was a slave, too."

What local residents refer to as the "slave house" is located to the west of the Shenandoah Farms office, off route 638, over in the field.

"When you look over in the field you'll see a big white house and then a barn. That house goes back before the Civil War. That house was there in slave time. That was where Uncle Travis' mother used to work for people named Rust. And Uncle Jim, he was just a boy, he lived there, too.

"The Yankee soldiers came by there looking for Mr. Charles Rust. She used to tell them he was over there in the mountains. Uncle Jim, he was just a little boy, standing there looking at the Yankees.

"One day they came by looking for the key to the meat house. She told them she didn't have the key, Mr. Rust had the key in his pocket. The leader of the Yankee soldiers he told his soldiers to grab a two by four, and they grabbed it and ran right against the door, about four of them. They knocked the door clean off the hinges.

"They went in there and got every scrap of bone meat they could get. Then, Uncle Jim said, they put it on their horses and went away to the mountains."

Charlie told of another time, according to his Uncle Jim, when the Yankees came by.

"The Rusts used to take their cattle up the mountain to graze. Well this one day they got them all up there except for this heifer. The Yankees came by and they were on their horses. They let out across the field after her, lasooed her, killed and butchered her and strapped the meat up and hung it on their horses and left."

"Uncle Jim said the Yankees were mad that every day they came they couldn't find Mr. Rust," Charlie said.

"Every time Mr. Rust heard the Yankees were coming he would go up in the mountains. One day they came and they found Mr. Rust. This Yankee Captain told his men to form a lane. Uncle Jim said Mr. Rust was forced to walk through it. He said it was the worst abuse he ever saw a man take."

Charlie Reynolds remembers that the "new era" for Blue Mountain started in 1951. It was in that year that the first house built by a "city person" went up on the mountain. Quite a marvelous house it was, too. This house was built five years before Henry and Colette de Longfief set their eyes on what they would later name Blue Mountain.

Today, the property is familiarly known to residents as the "Oulahan place." It is so close to Blue mountain (across the road from where the de Longfief's home is) that many people think it is part of Blue Mountain.

Charlie recalls that the land was purchased and a house was built on the property in 1951 by an Argentine Ambassador to Washington, Ambassador Ramos and Mrs. Ramos. The Ramos' purchased the property from Colonel Samuel Rolfe Miller of Front Royal.

The purchase of the Miller property by Ambassador Ramos introduced electricity, for the first time, to Blue Mountain.

"Up to that time the electric lines only extended up to my barn," Charlie said, pointing to his old red barn.

"Well, she wanted the line extended to her house and she paid me three hundred dollars to cut the line to her house."

Charley cut the line from his barn, up an old, unused road which runs behind his barn, through the forest and comes out on route 638 to the Ramos (now Oulahan) property.

The Ramos' house was the first of many beautiful mountain homes that were to rise on, or near, Blue Mountain in the years to come.

Diana McLellan, a reporter for the <u>Washington Star</u>, visited the home in the Spring of 1972 (after the Oulahans purchased it) and wrote a feature story about it. The <u>Star</u> presented her story in a full page spread, with pictures, in its June 1, 1972 issue. She wrote:

"Ear-popping high on the Virginia mountainside, with only the hum and twitter of the woods hanging in the clear air, sits the Courts Oulahans' house of paradoxes.

"It's an urbane country house. It's a house full of old treasures and young ideas. It's a Latin American house bustling with Irish-American hospitality. It's in the heart of collards-and-corn-puddin' country, and its chatelaine stirs her delicate Gallic sauces in antique French copper pots.

"A far cry from the bare-beamed, braid-rugged, knotty-pine syndrome of most second homes, the little villa to which the Washington lawyer and his family retreat from the summer swelter is a tiny polished jewel set on a croquet-smooth lawn among the violet-paved, steep sloping woods of Blue Mountain.

"It was built some 21 years ago by an Argentine ambassador to the United States and his wife."

When Henry de Longfief came to Blue Mountain in 1956, Charlie Reynolds was sixty-one years old.

"I was able to do a lot of work then. I felt good. I was real active. Not like I am now," Charlie said.

Charlie cut through the line bringing the electricity from the Ramos house to the first de Longfief home (now the cabin owned by Polly Frederick).

Charlie and his helper, Philip, helped build some of the first houses on Blue Mountain. They helped the Martins put up their house in 1958.

"That man. That Charlie Reynolds. He's one of the most wonderful people the Lord made. We're all thankful to him for just being Charlie Reynolds," Mrs. Marge Martin said in talking about Charlie.

Charlie Reynolds doesn't feel as good these days as he used to years ago.

But a lot of people still find their way up to Charlie's door to "set a spell," as Charlie says, and "talk about what's going on."

One day I was there and I told Charlie about the compliment Mrs. Martin paid him.

"Well, Mrs. Martin, she's nice folks. She's got the nicest laugh. I tell her I can hear her laughin', up there on the mountain, way down here in the holler. Mrs. Martin. Yes, I know her."

And then, Mrs. Reynolds, sitting there rocking on the porch, she chimes in:

"Yes, that Charlie, he knows everybody. He jus' knows everybody."

- 3 -
FINDING A "PLACE" AGAIN

I remember when I was growing up in Upstate New York that I treasured my family's trip to the Adirondack Mountains. That vast wilderness was so wild and so beautiful – so different from the routine daily life of the city. A significant event occurred in 1954. Three of my older brothers, knowing of the family's great love for the mountains, pooled their resources and bought a marvelous summer home in the mountains on one of those fresh, sparkling Adirondack lakes. What had been for me, up to then, an intermittent affair with the Adirondacks, now became a life-long love. I was in my twenties at the time and had just begun my career as a reporter on a newspaper. From then on I was in the Adirondacks on every occasion I could manage. I covered every event imaginable from sporting events to snow queen carnivals. And I wrote many feature articles about "the woods" from interviews with old guides and the early railroads to the stories of the great lodges built by the Vanderbilts and Morgans. It was the first time in my life when I fell in love with a "place". I had up to then limited my conception of love to people. I was surprised to find that I had a longing, deep within me, for quiet days spent by a cool lake, surrounded by evergreen trees.

Years later I came to Washington to be a correspondent for New York State newspapers. I liked the excitement and glamour of this new assignment. But one day the glamour wore off. I sensed something missing in my life. The "something missing" was my closeness to mountains, my accessibility in Upstate New York to our mountain home. I set out one day from Washington in search of a new mountain home, or at least a small lot to begin with. I was pleasantly surprised to find many mountain areas within a short driving distance from Washington – from the Catoctin mountains of Maryland, the Alleghenies of West Virginia to the Blue Ridge of Virginia. For two years from 1968 to 1970 I visited practically every mountain area and development within a hundred mile radius. What I was looking for, I realized later, was an exact replica of the Adirondack atmosphere that I had known as a child and a young adult. Time after time I would reject one development after another for various reasons. But the main reason, I found, was that few mountain communities maintained that naturalness that I was looking for. One community would bulldoze all the trees down so that what you had left was a barren piece of land with houses that belonged in the suburbs, but not on a mountain. Others had shoddy house contruction or trailers on blocks mixed in with regular houses. Somehow, I thought, it is all wrong. Isn't there any place that preserves nature – that builds houses that blend in with the forest?

One day in the Blue Ridge mountains of Virginia I found an affirmative answer to my long search. Where Virginia Route 55 cuts through the Blue Ridge is Manassas Gap. It is one of those historic gaps through which Southern troops poured on their way to the early battles of the Civil War. Up from the little crossroads community of Linden wound a dirt road that, a sign said, led to a place called Blue Mountain. I cannot remember the exact date I first went up that road, but it was probably in the spring of 1968, during the first year I had begun looking for mountain property. I had been used to coming on mountain developments more directly. This road seemed to wind interminably – up, up, winding up the mountain through the forest, brightened by dogwoods. My popping ears told me I was ascending a substantial mountain, at least for the Blue Ridge.

I finally found the information office, tucked away in enveloping trees. A short, smiling man was standing on the porch, his head cocked to one side, his hands on his hips.

"So, you have found us. Do you like what you see?" he said expectantly in a thick French accent.

This was my first meeting with Henry de Longfief – builder, writer, architect, salesman – but above all, the guiding genius of Blue Mountain.

"Henry," a friend of mine remarked years later, "has all of the Gallic charm of a Maurice Chevalier mixed with the infuriating stubbornness of a Charles de Gaulle."

This day he was all charm.

"Are you looking to buy property?" he said.

"Yes. Maybe. I don't know." I remember stuttering quite surprised, after my long drive, at finding this exuberant Parisian hidden away in the forest, waving his arms and talking to me in his animated manner.

"But, first," he said, "you must come and see the view. Shall we go in my car?"

We only went a short distance before we arrived at a very large structure.

"This is my restaurant. We will go there later. But first the view."

We walked down from the parking lot, through the grass, to the rocky area in front of the great structure. I wasn't prepared for what was to come. It was a clear, fresh Spring day.

The view was magnificent. Down below the green Shenandoah Valley spread until it reached the blue haze of the Alleghenies of West Virginia, forty miles away. In the Valley itself stood Masanutten, proud and strong, like a silent sentinel to all of the history that had swirled around it. The Shenandoah River, barely visible, wound its way, on its journey to Harper's Ferry, to meet the Potomac. The pictures of an early America came to mind. Where we stood Indians once trod. The pioneers saw this sight as the wagon trains rolled westward, and, at night, see those Civil War campfires, stretching the length of the Valley – soldiers resting for the battle.

Henry let me take in the view in silence. Words could not describe its powerful pull on the mind and the imagination.

I don't remember very much of the rest of my first visit to Blue Mountain that day. Henry showed me some lots that were for sale. I know I didn't make any decision to buy. I bid him good bye and went back down the winding dirt road.

For two more years I roamed the mountain areas of Virginia, Maryland and West Virginia, searching for my new mountain home. But I always found myself coming back to Blue Mountain, going up that winding road, talking again and again to that exuberant Frenchman.

I remember one day, after my fourth or fifth visit, Henry and I were walking in the woods. He took my arm, the way Europeans do, in a warm fatherly fashion.

"You know, Dick," he said in his accented voice, "you keep coming back to Blue Mountain. I think you are hooked!"

We both laughed.

In the Spring of 1970 I finally made a decision to buy a lot at Blue Mountain. The next year I built my mountain house there.

Henry was right. I was hooked.

Henry & Colette de Longfeif
Together they built a mountain kingdom of moderately priced
homes that did not disturb the beauty of the forest.

- 4 -
AU REVOIR HENRY DE LONGFIEF

Henry Villieras de Longfief died in a hospital in Front Royal, Virginia on August 31, 1975. He was 73 years old. Death was attributed to a heart attack.

I saw Henry the day he died. He and his wife, Colette, were sitting quietly together in the Blue Mountain Information Office. It was a beautiful day, with just a hint of coolness, the approach of autumn, in the air. It was the type of day that people love to spend at Blue Mountain. A good day for hiking, or sitting by the fire.

I was expecting a large group of friends up from Washington. I wanted to put up an additional direction sign at one of the Blue Mountain crossroads to make sure they found my place. I stopped by to see Henry and tell him what I was doing.

"Of course, of course, no problem," he said as he gave his approval to putting up the sign.

In the seven years that I had known Henry we had had our good times and our bad times. We had had shouting matches. I had wanted to build a shed in the rear of my house once.

"You cannot do that," he thundered. "It is prohibited by our covenants. Anyway sheds turn into shacks. Here," he pointed, his anger subsiding a bit, "build it underneath your house, so it won't be noticed."

I was furious. I had planned on that shed for months. But, in the long run, I had to agree. Henry had a point. He was vociferous when he felt he was saving his beloved Blue Mountain's natural beauty from desecration. He would always get you with this type of line:

"Why did you choose Blue Mountain? You liked what you saw, right? You didn't see any trailers or shacks. You saw nice little houses, blending in with the forest."

Henry was forever the teacher. We, who lived at Blue Mountain, whether we were generals, doctors, writers or government bureaucrats, were always the pupils, whether we liked it or not.

After my experience about the shed a fellow Blue Mountain home owner commiserated with me.

"So, he said, "You've had a little battle with the terrible Frenchman.

"What you don't understand," he said, with a humorous glint in his eye, "is that when you bought a lot at Blue Mountain you became part of a medieval kingdom. Henry is the Lord and Master. We are his fiefs. All we need at Blue Mountain is a drawbridge."

In interviewing people at Blue Mountain for this book I learned that everyone had a story to tell about Henry. They had all had at least one battle with him. But, amazingly, most people spoke about him with great affection. What they most admired about him was his devotion to his forest kingdom, Blue Mountain.

"You know," home owner Johnny Clark said, "Henry was a man of vision. He had this sense of what a mountain community should be like. And he was a strong man. No one was going to ruin this vision."

Other people became so infuriated with what they considered Blue Mountain's strict regulations that, soon after buying a lot at Blue Mountain, and after their first confrontation with Henry, they left, sold their lot, and were never heard from again.

On a recent visit to Blue Mountain I had introduced a friend to several of my neighbors. Later, back at my place, he said:

"This fellow, Henry. Is he dead?"

"Yes," I said. "Why do you ask?"

"Well the way people talk about him up here – 'Henry said this' 'Henry did this' Why you would think he was still alive."

I was amused by the observation. I had never thought about it. But it was true. Other recent visitors said the same thing. I couldn't figure it out. But then one day it came to me. Henry had such a strong effect on all of our lives, that it was like he was still alive. We had all (at varying times) loved him, hated him, feared him. He was like a father to us. Once in a while praising us. But, many times, scolding us.

And even on this day that I visited him for the last time, I thought that my visit was two-fold. I always liked to meet him, even though I could never count on what his mood would be. He had an intense, electric personality. He was very much the type of person who lived in the present moment, savoring it, whether it brought joy or anger. Living it.

But another purpose of my visit was to seek permission to put up my small directional sign. As I think back Henry had trained me and others well. Even these small details. He was to be informed or, you might feel his wrath.

So, even on this last day, my emotions toward him were mixed. Affection and fear.

He looked, as usual, healthy, pink-cheeked, ten to fifteen years younger than his age. Yet, everyone knew, he did the work of three men everyday.

"Henry," I said. "You look great."

"Thank you, Dick," he said. "That is nice of you to say that. But I do not feel so good today."

It was, as I recall now, one of the few times that I heard him give an indication that he was not feeling well.

"He is working too hard. He always works too hard," his wife, Colette, said.

I introduced a friend, Walter Carroll, who was with me. This friend and I had been reporters in another city, at one time.

"Oh, a reporter, I have been that, too," Henry said.

I told my friend that Henry had been a White House correspondent for a French news agency during the days when Franklin D. Roosevelt was president.

"There was no television then," Henry said. "It was before World War II. The President would call us into his office for a chat. It was more informal then. But those were exciting times, too."

Part of Henry's charm was that he could relate to many people because he had done so many things. It all helped in "selling" Blue Mountain.

When, on my first visit, I told him that I was, for much of my life, a newspaperman, he told me about his own journalism experience in Paris and Washington.

But Henry had also been a teacher, a builder, an architect, an electricia, a realtor, a businessman. He also had an avid interest in a whole range of subjects: history, painting, geology, (he and his wife, Colette, are rockhounds) archeology. So, I could see any number of people from those professions and interests, on their first visit to Blue Mountain, relating to Henry in a very personal way.

Colette said she remembers when they were growing up in France that Henry "always talked about coming to America."

"He was always reading about this country. He was amazed at the opportunities available here. One of the books he liked was a biography of Henry Ford. He read many other books about America. But he was especially impressed by biographies of self-made men, like Henry Ford and Thomas Edison and others."

I had always been fascinated by the de Longfiefs' attraction to mountain living.

"Oh, this goes back a long time, in Europe, back before we were married," Colette said.

"We loved to go on hikes together and, of course, we are rockhounds and we like to look for new finds."

For years, before and after they were married, they hiked and camped in mountains in France, Spain and Italy.

For a long time both of them had been involved in the journalistic and writing world of Paris. Henry was a reporter on "Le Petit Parisien". Colette contributed articles on the theatre. In 1937 Henry was impressed by an article in his own newspaper about the great desire of Americans to learn French.

"This was what gave us the impetus to come to this country," Colette said.

They began their school, a correspondence course in French, in New York City in 1937. They were successful for awhile but they ran into some hard times in 1939. At this time Henry returned to journalism and got a job as a reporter with HA VAS, a French news agency in New York. Shortly afterward, he became the new service's Washington correspondent assigned to the White House.

When America became involved in World War II he joined the press staff of General Charles De Gaulle, first in North Africa and later in France.

When he returned to America in 1945, after the war, he began a new venture as a real estate salesman in Arlington. At this point Henry's talents as a salesman came to the fore. He estimated, that during one period, he was selling a house every day.

"He realized then," Colette said, "that he could go into business for himself. This was a period when he got great confidence in himself. Later on he decided that he was going to be a builder. He designed a model house in Falls Church which won the House of the Year Award."

The de Longfiefs were in the real estate and building business in Arlington for more than 10 years.

"But, we were both getting tired of that type of existence," Colette said. "I longed for the days when we used to go hiking in the mountains of Europe. At least, I told Henry, let us look for an acre or two of mountain land, to go to on the weekends. He agreed that it was a good idea."

So, in the middle 1950s, the de Longfiefs began to look around at the mountain areas of Virginia and Maryland. I was surprised to find how closely their search resembled my own.

"We used to enjoy the rides into the country," Colette said, "but we had a very difficult time finding what we wanted. I think we had an image in our mind of a small cabin, surrounded by trees. But what we found were developments where, in some cases they had removed all of the trees. The houses looked like the ones in a suburb. Other times we would find that the trees remained but the houses were too close together, of shoddy construction and sometimes they had houses and trailers all lumped together. Somehow, it seemed all wrong. It wasn't what we wanted."

The de Longfiefs' long search was valuable to them, tho. They learned what they didn't like. Those ideas became incorporated into the strict covenants of Blue Mountain.

"Then, one day," Colette recalls, with a certain pleasant look coming to her eyes, "we went up this old dirt road. We really didn't know where it was leading us. But it seemed to be a very old, untouched part of America. We loved this mountain from the day we rode up here. It had such beautiful views."

The de Longfiefs found that the mountain belonged to an old lumberman, James McDonald. Many years ago McDonald had lumbered the mountain. He owned approximately 800 acres, most of it on top of the mountain, much of it with spectacular views of the Shenandoah Valley down below.

"Henry asked Mr. McDonald if he could buy an acre or two," Colette said. "But he wasn't interested. He wanted to sell us the whole thing, eight hundred acres. Henry said, "No." But then I thought a while and said, "Wait.""

This is essentially how the de Longfiefs bought a mountain. They later called it Blue Mountain.

Cornell Stoots, Administrative Assistant at Blue Mountain for over 20 years.

Blue Mountain home of author Dick Long. Built in 1971.

- 5 -
BLUE MOUNTAIN–
CLOSE TO AMERICAN HISTORY

"These two men, they stood at the apex of American history. And their stories evolved not too far from Blue Mountain."

The speaker was Henry de Longfief. And his hands were waving as he was talking. It was one of my more pleasant days at Blue Mountain. Henry's chores were finished for the day. He had stopped by my mountain home to inspect my new deck that his men had just constructed. But soon, like a lot of his visits, he was talking about something else.

Henry, who was an omnivorous reader, was absorbed by American History. The 'two men' he was talking about that day were George Washington and Lord Fairfax.

After Henry died, his widow, Colette, told me: "When we were younger, in Paris, he read all about America. He was amazed that there was so much opportunity here. You know, we both worked on newspapers. So we met many Americans who visited or worked in Paris. He constantly questioned them about this country."

Henry was thrilled that the mountain that he had purchased was surrounded by American History. He related how Washington, as a 17-year-old surveyor was hired by Lord Fairfax, who owned 8 million acres of Virginia land, including what became Blue Mountain.

"The first meeting of Washington and Lord Fairfax was only a short distance from Blue Mountain," Henry said. Some historians say the visit took place near Howellsville, before Fairfax moved to Greenway Court. Washington, as a surveyor, could have been in the Blue Mountain area on several occasions.

It is known that he passed through here, crossed the Shenandoah River, as a British soldier in the fateful French and Indian war

Henry's interest in local history spurred me on to increase my knowledge, too.

Lord Fairfax, whose tomb is in Winchester, was an interesting figure in Colonial American history. He was true English nobility and grew up in Leeds Castle. He was educated at Oxford and acquired a substantial library, much of which was transferred to his estate at Greenway Court, near Winchester. But, in his days at Oxford, he preferred to ride horses and hunt with his fellow students. Thus, in his years here, he loved to do the same in the Virginia countryside.

This huge grant of Virginia land to Lord Fairfax was a royal grant from the King of England. It caused a lot of friction between Lord Fairfax and the Colonial Virginia government. The government in Williamsburg didn't like this huge royal presence who was eating up property money in quit rents that would normally go to the government.

It was interesting to note that when the American Revolution drove the English back to England, Lord Fairfax, who didn't care for the Colonial government didn't want to go back to England. He lived out his final years here in Virginia.

Henry de Longfief was especially interested in the influence of the older Lord Fairfax on the 17-year-old Washington, who was a surveyor at the time.

"Remember," Henry said, "Lord Fairfax had this big library at his home right here in rural Virginia. I can see the young Washington reading there at Greenway Court. It was like a father-son relationship, I think."

Blue Mountain is approximately 65 miles west of Washington, it can be reached by routes 66 and 55 – the Washington to Front Royal routes. On this approach the traveler would take route 638 up the mountain from Linden. Another route, a little longer, would be route 50 (the Washington to Winchester route), up route 638 from that direction, just before it reached the Shenandoah River. Route 638 runs north and south, weaving through the heart of Blue Mountain. Two historic Blue Ridge Mountain gaps – Manassas Gap on the south and Ashby Gap on the north serve as border marks, not only for the Blue Mountain area, but also for the general geographical area that concerns this book.

Ashby Gap, near the picturesque community of Paris, Virginia, is the entranceway through which a young George Washington first visited the Blue Ridge Mountains and Shenandoah Valley in 1748. Also, Ashby gap and Manassas Gap (Linden) played crucial roles in the Civil War. Thousands of Southern and Northern troops marched through these gaps on their way (at various times) to such historic Civil War battles as Bull Run, Antietam and Gettysburg.

When young Washington came out to the mountains for the first time, it was estimated that he made 40 miles by horseback over pioneer trails from Mount Vernon in one day. The reason for Washington's journey was interesting. Lord Fairfax, a friend of the Washington family, had been granted, from the King of England, five million acres of Virginia land. But the wealthy English Lord was wary of what he considered poachers on his land. Thus he asked his cousin, George Fairfax who lived at his estate, Belvoir, (near Mount Vernon) to come out to the Valley to help him survey his land. Fairfax brought along George Washington, then 16 years old.

Lord Fairfax's residence or "quarter," at this time was on the east bank of the Shenandoah River, somewhere in the vicinity of Howellsville, at the foot of Blue Mountain. On March 12, 1748 the two Georges – Washington and Fairfax went through Ashby's Gap, descended to the Shenandoah and went south to meet Lord Fairfax. This famous meeting, between Lord Fairfax and George Washington, took place in the shadow of Blue Mountain. The young Washington, in the months and years to come, was to be employed as a surveyor for Lord Fairfax. It is a strong possibility that Washington surveyed Blue Mountain in the middle 1700s as the mountain as well as hundreds of thousands of nearby acres was the property of Lord Fairfax.

Washington, for the next ten years, was to roam the mountains and the valley of Virginia as surveyor and later military leader, especially near Winchester, the experiences gained in these younger years in the mountains would profit him immeasurably as the military leader of the American Revolution.

Lord Fairfax, shortly after his first meeting with Washington, was to move into his new residence at Greenway Court. As the crow flies, Greenway Court is seven miles west of Blue Mountain, in the Valley. It is easy for the mind to speculate on the influence Lord Fairfax had on the young Washington. At the time the Oxford-educated Fairfax, a bachelor, was 43 years old, living on an estate in the wilds of Virginia. This estate, Greenway Court, had an excellent library. To this place came all of the important personages of that day in Virginia. The effect on the young Washington must have been powerful.

But beyond the Washington-Fairfax connection, I found in my research several other fascinating historical aspects.

- The land where Henry and Colette de Longfief built their house was once owned by a confederate officer who was wounded at Antietam, the bloodiest battle of the Civil War.

- The mountain, like many lovely, isolated places, was a refuge for "deserters" or "runaways" of all descriptions.

- I found that the mountain had a large black population at one time. Why? Escaped slaves, before and after the Civil War, fled here and found safety.

- Mosby's Rangers, the famed Southern guerilla fighters, would escape to Blue Mountain, in between their raids on Yankee supply lines.

- When I was talking to one old timer he was talking about "deserters" from the Army escaping to the mountain. I presumed he was referring to the Civil War.

  I said: "Which side, North or South?":

  "Oh, no," he said, "not that war. The Revolutionary War." I was stunned.

  I have not pinned down definite information on that, yet, but I did learn that there were deserters from both the British and American sides in the Virginia area. And one group, the Hessians, who were mercenaries for the British, liked America so much, they stayed on in the nearby Shenandoah Valley and felt very much at home with the Pennsylvania Germans who had settled parts of the Valley.

- One day I visited an apple orchard, Freezeland Orchard, which adjoins the Blue Mountain property. Because the visitor, by car, only sees a few trees, I thought the orchard was a small operation.

  I found that the orchard contained 20,000 trees and encompassed an area of 800 acres, about the size of Blue Mountain. Also it was owned by a family whose roots go back into the earliest days of American history. The orchard was founded in 1906 – the year when Henry de Longfief was a four-year-old toddler in Paris. The apples from this orchard, amazingly, were first purchased (before World War I) by England. Later, they found a market in Argentina.

- I found in my travels around, talking to older people, that some wonderful Appalachian types lived on the mountain many years ago. It was lumbered at the turn of the century and beyond. The abundance of apple and peach trees on the mountain made wonderful moonshine – "white lightning" – I was told. Families grew up on the mountain – storing their food in spring houses, slaughtering hogs in the fall, riding their horses on the old lumber roads, singing their mountain ballads.

This journey of mine began nearly forty years ago when, for the first time, I went up that winding dirt road to Blue Mountain. It was a pleasant trip then, and it continues to be today.

- 6 -
LUMBERING AT BLUE MOUNTAIN, OR-OLD MCDONALD HAD A FARM

*In 1915, Ruth McDonald Mitchell, daughter of lumberman James McDonald, was
brought as a baby to what would later become Blue Mountain. She recalls growing up
on the mountain in Appalachian style living as one of ten children.*

The story of Blue Mountain at the turn of the century is the story of a lumberman by the name of James McDonald.

Jim McDonald's mark is still on Blue Mountain. Look closely at any area of the forest and you will see large stumps. Some of these stumps represent giant trees that were felled ninety years ago. Blue Mountain is known as a second growth forest. A visitor to the mountain sixty years ago would have seen a barren land of stumps. There were also, (strange as it seems today) large areas of rich, green pasture, where cattle grazed.

A living witness to the Blue Mountain of seventy years ago is Mrs. Ruth McDonald Mitchell. Born in 1915, she is one of 10 children born to James and Belle McDonald.

"It was a beautiful place back in there when I was a child" she said. "I can just close my eyes and know what it looked like. Why, there weren't any trees then. Just beautiful green pasture. I can remember running barefoot through the fields, right there where they have the information office now."

Ruth McDonald Mitchell, as a baby, was carried to Blue Mountain in her mother's arms.

"It must have been nineteen-fifteen, the year I was born, when I was taken up there. I was suckin' the bottle – I was still nursin' – when I was taken up there by my mother."

Her father, James McDonald, was born a few miles from Blue Mountain in 1874. He married Belle McDonald in 1898. The McDonalds, as a family, have lived in the Howellsville-Front Royal area (as far as can be determined) for more than 150 years. The McDonalds are an important, direct link in Blue Mountain history. Henry de Longfief bought the land that is now Blue Mountain (approximately 800 acres) from Jim McDonald in 1956. McDonald died, at the age of 85, in Linden on January 2, 1959.

Mrs. Mitchell's memories of Blue Mountain span nearly 70 years and comprise a fascinating look at Appalachian Mountain living long ago. It was a time of simple living: lumbering, hog-butchering, moonshiners (there were two legal distilleries, and several illegal stills in Blue Mountain's early history), farming, one-room school houses, no electricity, horse and buggies, and six-mule teams hauling logs out of the woods.

The old McDonald home was just a few hundred feet from Deer Lake, where present day Blue Mountaineers go swimming. The old house, vacant for many years, had fallen into disrepair over the years. It was torn down by Blue Mountain in 1975. It is presently a picnic area with tables, near the lake parking lot.

Mrs. Mitchell remembers three early houses in the general area of the present day information office. The previously mentioned McDonald home (by the parking lot), another house stood on the site of the present-day Deer Lake. This house and land owned once by the George H. Sawers family (among others) was torn down to make way for the lake. Still another house stood on the land now occupied by the de Longfief home. This was once owned by Francis Lehew, a Confederate officer. This house was occupied by a Bill Rosenberry around the turn of the century. Also, nearly in the same era, was the site of a legal distillery that made apple jack and peach brandy.

"We all lived up there, at one time or another," Mrs Mitchell said of the large McDonald family.

"After my father married my mother they lived at his father's home. That house was near Blue Mountain. Then later on they moved to the top of the mountain."

(Mrs. Mitchell isn't exactly sure but she thinks her father and mother moved to their mountain home about 1910. This is probably correct as records in the Warren County Couthouse list a transfer of property from George H. Sawers (previous owner of the land) to James McDonald on May 27, 1910.)

"After he moved to the mountain he bought one place at a time," she said. He didn't buy all of that land at one time. At that time the land was very very cheap. Just a coupla' dollars an acre. He was a sawmill man, a lumber man and that's what he made his livin' in, was sawin' lumber.

"He would buy one place and saw the timber off'n that and then he would see another place that he wanted that had good timber on it and he would buy that."

A review of the transfer of the poperty (in Warren County Courthouse) between James McDonald and Henry de Longfief reflects this pattern many years later. The Blue Mountain purchase was not one sale of 800 acres. It represented more than 15 separate purchases of McDonald properties that ranged between 25 acres and 97 acres, that added up to the grand total of about 800 acres.

Mrs. Mitchell said her father, at one time, owned 3300 acres of mountain and forest land.

"But the Blue Mountain property was always our home. He always returned there. This was our home," she said.

The turn-of-the-century lumbermen had portable, steam sawmills they transported to various parts of the forest, wherever the job was to be done. The lumber crews traveled from site-to-site, too. Temporary quarters (shantys) would be built in the forest that served as places for the men to eat and live. From time to time present day Blue Mountaineers will report seeing what they think are the remains of an old house in the forest. Many of these are what is left of the old lumber shanties.

Also, what look like old roads in the forest, are the original lumber roads formed by horses and mules pulling the lumber out of the forests on wagons.

"The lumber would be hauled out on wagons drawn by horses. My father also had a six-mule team that brought the lumber out," she said.

That part of route 638 that winds through Blue Mountain going north (generally) to Linden is an old lumber road formed by the McDonald wagons, horses and mules pulling out the logs, over the years. The present-day route 638 was made into a suitable dirt road by the Civilian Conservation Corps (CCC) in 1933, as part of President Franklin Roosevelt's public works projects.

"My father gave the government the land so that the CCC's could build the road," Mrs. Mitchell said.

But, long before she saw the CCCs work on the Howellsville to Linden road, she remembers Blue Mountain as a very special place in her childhood. She spent the first ten years of her life, from 1915 to 1925, at the family home near the present day Deer Lake.

"We had a garden, and cows to milk, we had a regular farm there."

"All of us children grew up, up there. There were eleven of us. But one died so that made ten of us. So its not like we were lonesome. There was always somethin' to do. But it was not like today. There was no radio – no TV, no electricity. We used oil lamps. We'd pick raspberries and huckleberries and my mother would can them and we would store them in our springhouse."

"It was a farm there as we growed all of our own food. And we also had to grow the food to feed the men in the sawmill camps. Those men were movin' around the mountain all the time. My father would see a piece of timber that had to be cut and he'd move the men to that part of the mountain. They would bring the sawmill with them. Then they would build a lumber shanty and the men would live there. They would stay there and have their meals there. They would stay overnight during the week nights. Some of them would go back to their families on weekends. When all of the timber was cut they would move on to another piece of timber in another part of the mountain, build a lumber shanty and start all over again."

It was also the days of the horse and buggy.

"There weren't any cars, then," she recalled. "If we ever went any place we'd go by horse and buggy. And when my father would move to a new place on the mountain, for the sawin', they had to use horses. They had to haul their lumber on wagons. And when we went to the store my mother would hook up the horse and buggy. We would all ride in the buggy."

"We raised hogs, too. And the hogs would run wild over the mountain. Then we would catch them in the Fall. We would butcher seven or eight hogs in the Fall. Then we would salt the hogs. The pork would be salted and this would last us through the winter."

They had their own natural "refrigerator."

"We kept all of our food in a Springhouse," she said. "The Springhouse was down by the lake. There was no lake then. But there were springs there and we would put the food in the springhouse and this would keep it nice and fresh and cool during the summer months, or anytime, for that matter."

In the tradition of Appalachia "moonshine" (illegal whisky) was made on Blue Mountain many years ago. The mountain was also the site of two legal distilleries – one called Brandy Camp (about half way between the Blue Mountain information office and Howellsville – off 638) and the other was located in the general area of the present day de Longfief home.

"They would make moonshine in the mountains," Mrs. Mitchell said when talking about the illegal kind.

"Of course there was a time when it was legal, when they made it at the Brandy Camp, near Howellsville. But then when the state of Virginia went dry, well they made the white lightnin' up on Blue Mountain."

She was about nine or ten years old when she first recalled the "moonshinin." That would have been about 1925.

"They'd make it in several places on the mountain. They could make it out of peaches or apples. They'd set the mash, then run it off into the still. They'd put the sugar in the mash – whatever you'd want to make it with apples or peaches – in big barrels, then you let that 'work' and it sours and then they set up their still, and it has to be copper – so that it doesn't poison anyone – it has to be copper – so they cook this mash and it runs off through a 'worm' a copper tubing shaped like a worm, then it goes through the cold water, then it runs out into a jug, and they call this 'singlin."

"Why do they call it 'singling,' I asked.

"Well, that's the first ones they'd make, to see how it tastes. If it was OK they pour it back in and then they'd start making a batch."

Mrs. Mitchell said "white lightnin'" was made in "four or five places" on Blue Mountain in the old days.

"Of course, they'd have to have a place where there was water. So it was made near the springs usually.

"If they made a whole lot they would put it in these wooden kegs – these five gallon kegs. Or they'd bottle it in glass jars."

The moonshine was either sold by the keg or the jars to people who would come up the mountain.

She remembers many times the "revenuers" (federal or state agents) would come up the mountain and "cut up the stills."

"So the moonshiners had to be careful who they sold it to so's they wouldn't get turned in or have the stills cut up."

She remembers when they were "workin' the lightnin'" they would put a guard on the only road leading up the mountain (now 638).

She remembers the first cars in the Blue Mountain area in the 1920's.

"The cars didn't have no trouble gettin' to Howellsville. But the road up the mountain was pretty rough. There was a big rock and they couldn't get by that. So some of them would go up this field and get here that way. This field ended up where we lived. Of course after the CCC's built that road, you could go anywhere then."

Mrs. Mitchell remembers walking four miles a day (both ways) to a little one-room schoolhouse. The school no longer exists but it was located in what is now forest about half-way between Blue Mountain's information office and Howellsville.

"It's all growed up now. But all that area from Blue Mountain to Howellsville was all pasture land then," she said.

When she was ten years old (in 1925) she remembers that the family moved to Howellsville.

"My folks wanted the children to have as much education as possible. And the school for the older kids was located in Howellsville," she said.

(In recent years there has been some confusion about the location of Howellsville. Many persons today refer to Howellsville as the intersection of routes 638 and 603 where the Shenandoah Farms Grocery store is located. Actually much of Howellsville is hidden from the eye. If you take the road where the sign stating "Howellsville Methodist Church" is standing it will lead you to the "main" part of Howellsville.)

The McDonald's brother, Marvin, his wife and children live in the house that fronts on route 603. This house was once a store and was owned by Frank Oliver.

Mrs. Mitchell has many happy memories of the nearby Howellsville Methodist church.

"My great grand mother went to that church," she recalled.

Her sister? Mrs. Daisy McDonald Berry left $11,000 in her will to renovate the church. (There are several McDonalds and their relations buried in the small cemetery next to the church.)

The McDonald family still owns tracts of land adjacent to Blue Mountain. Mrs. Mitchell and her husband were left an 85-acre tract that is generally to the west of what is known as the "old Trail" road to Paris, Virginia. They use this land to graze their cattle. There is an old house there that belonged to the Cox family. On a recent visit there Mrs. McDonald pointed to a pile of rocks and said, "That is the foundation of the old slave house."

She said the house pre-dated the Civil War and was where "slaves lived."

About fifty yards away is an old family cemetery where 13 people are buried, including Jared McDonald, her great uncle and Sam Cox, a relative, both Confederate soldiers.

- 7 -
THE MARTINS -
BLUE MOUNTAIN CIRCA 1958

"Well, when we went back to Washington and told people we paid two thousand dollars for a bunch of trees, no water, unimproved property with no road on it – they said, 'Why you've lost your mind.' They thought we'd gone crazy."

As she tells how she and her husband bought one of the first lots at Blue Mountain, Marge Martin relates the story with relish.

"But you know what? We just had a ball up here in the beginning. Everett (her late husband) just couldn't wait to get up here. We used to live in the Kenwood section outside of Washington. The people there all go to the country club. Well, we'd had enough of that type of thing. We wanted our little acre in the mountains and we had it."

The Blue Mountain that Marge Martin is describing is circa 1958. The Martins purchased one of the first lots at Blue Mountain and were the first lot owners to erect a house. (The de Longfiefs had built their own house in 1956. It is now owned by Polly Frederick.)

Born in Chatanooga, Mrs. Martin met her future husband there and both had a love for the mountains of Tennessee.

"Everett went to the University of Tennessee at Knoxville and I used to visit him there and we would go camping and hiking in the Great Smoky Mountains. I guess we always loved mountains."

He was in the Navy in World War II and later as a civilian he was an electrical engineer with the Department of the Navy in Washington.

"Everett was forty and I was thirty-eight when our first and only child, Jo, was born," she related.

"We'd done all the glorious things in life, a lot of traveling, living in big cities. We lived in San Francisco and liked that very much. I think we were at the time in life when we wanted something else. We had a yearning for the mountains. We had come down to this area a lot, picnicking and hiking around the Skyline Drive and the Appalachian Trail.

"I think we knew we were looking for four or five acres, if we could only find it."

Mrs. Martin remembers it must have been when Jo was about three or four years old.

"Everett was reading the Sunday papers. He spotted this ad about Blue Mountain. He said, 'Let's go see it.' So we all got in the car, Everett, Jo, his mother and myself, and headed off to the mountains."

She remembers that the directions then used to route people down route 50, left on 638, and along the river.

"It was a September day in 1958," she recalls.

"It was so pretty then. There were hardly any houses at all. Shenandoah Farms didn't exist then. We went down along the river. We got to that point where the store is now, at Howellsville, but there was no store then, so quiet, just a sign there, giving directions.

"So we kept going, we kept driving up this road, and it was much worse than it is now. No place to turn around or to have a picnic lunch. Finally we made it to where the Information Office is now. And across from there was this shack. Well, this was their office."

She remembers that the de Longfiefs and Herbert Bryan (an early partner of the de Longfiefs) were there.

"Also this Mrs. Bolger, who was a saleswoman, she came out to greet us. We asked her if there was any place to picnic. She directed us to the area where the old house (the McDonald home) was, that's now torn down. They had some picnic trables there and we spread out our picnic lunch.

"A little later Mrs. Bolger came down to see us. She wanted to know if we were interested in buying property. We told her we were looking for four or five acres."

Mrs. Martin remembers that at that t time there was only one section of Blue Mountain open and surveyed into lots. That is the area across from the Information Office. The streets in there are: Black Walnut Lane, Dogwood Lane and Little Indian Trail.

"As I remember they said several of the lots in this area had been sold," she said.

"I looked at Everett and I could see the wheels churning around inside. We went back to the office."

When they got to the office, Mrs. Martin remembers her husband saying:

"Now, Margy, you stay in the car. I'll handle this. I don't want anyone pressuring me into buying a lot."

"I replied, 'Yes, Everett.' I really didn't know what he was going to do. Well, we waited and waited. I walked Jo back and forth to keep her happy. Mother was getting tired.

"Finally, Everett came back with a piece of paper and said 'Here, sign here.'

"I said, 'Everett, you didn't buy that lot.'

"'Yep, I bought that lot,' he replied."

Mrs. Martin, who lives by herself today in her home on Dogwood Lane, reflected on twenty years at Blue Mountain.

"Oh, it's been pure fun -- all the way, right from the start.

"When we first came up to clear the lot, Everett was as happy as a clam to get out into the woods. We came up every weekend. Jo was four years old then, in the beginning.

"You know she grew up, coming to Blue Mountain. She's married now and I was talking to her on the phone the other day and she said: 'Mother, don't ever sell that place, it's a part of my life.' I think it was good for all of us."

Their first year at Blue Mountain the Martins spent camping out in a tent.

"The de Longfiefs let us use their tent. It was the tent they used when they first came up here. We put a platform down and we got cots and lanters. And, when we weren't there, a lot of Everett's bachelor friends would come up and use it on the weekends.

"We kept clearing the land and Henry found some men to help us saw the larger trees."

But even in that first year the Martins were thinking about building a house at Blue Mountain.

"There were really only two houses up here then that people were living in – the de Longfiefs had their house and the Ramos – he was the Argentine ambassador – they had their house which is where the Oulahans live now," she said.

"First we said we would just use our lot for tenting, for weekends. Well, we couldn't stand it. We just had to have a house. But we didn't have any money. So we went around to the banks and they just laughed at us. They wouldn't give us any money. Oh, they would give us a personal loan, but not on a second home. Why, they said, back in 1927 that's what went first, those second homes, people just reneged on them.

"We kept thinking it over. We had an insurance policy that was coming due. So that's how we did it. We cashed it in and that gave us enough to start."

When the Martins built their house Henry de Longfief had not yet founded Blue Mountain Construction Co. He was not in the building business.

But, did Henry have any ideas about how their house should be built, I asked.

Mrs. Martin roared with laughter.

"Did he have ideas? Oh, my gosh, he was breathing down our neck every time we turned around, telling us what to do," she laughed.

"He wasn't concerned about the inside but he was about the outside. The house had to be on these poles. It couldn't be on cinder blocks. And there would be no colored houses at Blue Mountain. 'No, no, no.'" she said as she imitated with gestures, how Henry would talk.

"Why I remember this colonel who lived nearby here. He had cleared his lot. He was putting in cinder blocks. Henry had apoplexy. He wouldn't let him do it. He kept shouting, 'no, no, no.' Well, the colonel got mad, too. He sold his lot and never came back.

"And Sally Hazlett. They painted her house barn red and Henry had a fit," she related.

When Blue Mountaineers have nothing to talk about they start recounting their experiences with Henry when they started to build their houses. The conversation is usually mixed with gales of laughter – the familiar story of the new land owner, contemplating his dream house and running into the stubborn Frenchman who has very set ideas about how Blue Mountain should be developed. The Martins were the first of a long line of people who would recount their sometimes humorous, sometimes frightening experiences with Henry de Longfief.

"Henry designed the outside of the building. We had just a shell for along time.

"We got Charlie Reynolds and Phillip to help us. And they had this long-handled equipment for digging the post holes to put the posts in.

"And every once in a while they would hit a rock and Phillip would get down and start talking to the rock and he would say, in his high-pitched voice, 'Now big boy, you just move.'

"We had the best time. It was so much fun."

Eventually the house went up.

"Well we practically started the mountain. After our house was up why people came by like flies. And Henry was so proud and excited and he would point and say, 'See, people are living here.'"

Everett Martin died of cancer in April of 1976.

"He was in such good health all of his life, that it came as a shock. He had retired and we were both looking forward to coming here.

"There were two things he wanted in life. One was to see Jo graduate from college. The other was to come up on this mountain and stay."

The Martin place today is one of the most beautiful on Blue Mountain. Wide picture windows look out and down into the Shenandoah Valley. The fireplace, the rustic, comfortable furniture, give a feeling of a happy, lived-in home.

"My daughter and I spent last winter here (1976-77) and let me tell you it was a rough one. New Years night the line from the well froze. We didn't have water. Then the lights went out. Then, the car wouldn't start. But Charlie Smith (a neighbor) came along and pulled us out. You know we've got quite a community up on this mountain. We help eachother out. You have to have this spirit if you want to live here."

A LINK WITH THE CIVIL WAR

*Mrs. Frances Jett can see the blue haze on Blue Mountain from her home in the
Shenandoah Valley near Middletown. Her grandfather used to own grazing
land on Blue Mountain at the turn of the century.*

An old stone house in the Shenandoah valley is part of the horse-and-buggy past of Blue Mountain. The house also links the Mountain with a confederate hero of the Civil War.

"I remember running through the fields behind the house when I was a little girl. I would follow after my grandfather all the time as he supervised our farm. Sometimes we would look off in the distance and see those beautiful mountains. I could see the pasture land up in the mountain where we brought our cattle to graze in the Springtime."

The speaker of these words is Mrs. Frances Jett. The time she is talking about is more than 70 years ago, at the turn-of-the-century. Her grandfather is the late Captain Francis Lesley Lehew,

Captain of Company B, 17th Virginia Infantry, Confederate States of America. Captain Lehew, who owned the land where the de Longfief home is located, was wounded at Antietam, Maryland, in September of 1862, in the bloodiest battle of the Civil War.

The old stone house stands today in the Shenandoah Valley (north of Front Royal, near Cedarville) facing Blue Mountain, seven miles away, as it has done for nearly 160 years. Blue Mountain is quite visible from this spot as it is the mountain directly ahead with the towers on top. The house itself is called "Fairview," aptly named because of its excellent view of the mountains.

"My grandfather was married just after the Civil War. He brought his wife, my grandmother, to 'Fairview' on Christmas Eve, 1872. My mother was two years old then. I was born in that house on September 9, 1908. So it has a lot of memories."

Mrs. Jett could not recall the exact date that Captain Lehew bought the Blue Mountain land.

"But it must have been in the 1880's. It was a grim time here in the Valley, after the war. People didn't have much. So it must have been some time later that he bought the land."

Captain Lehew, as Mrs. Jett remembers, never lived at Blue Mountain.

"He had cattle and he had to have land for them to graze on. There was pasture land on the mountain. So he bought that land for grazing." she said.

She remembers as a child that she could look off in the distance and see the pasture land on Blue Mountain, seven miles away.

"As long as I can remember my grandfather would take his cattle up there every Springtime and bring them back in the Fall. It was a big undertaking, requiring a lot of men. There was always a lot of activity, preparing for the trip," she said.

It is interesting to look at a map of the Shenandoah Valley and the Blue Ridge Mountains and follow the route of the cattle to the mountain. It gives one more of a feeling of how these two entities are related. Although the distance from the Lehew home in the Valley to the Lehew property at Blue Mountain is seven miles, as the crow flies, it is about nine or ten miles using the route traveled by the cattle. The cattle would be driven in a southeasterly direction to the area of the west bank of the Shenandoah river. They would travel along the bank of the river until they reached "Morgan Ford." This is an old ford in the river that goes back to pre-Civil War days. (Motorists today use the low-lying bridge over Morgan Ford on route 624 to cross the Shenandoah.) After the cattle crossed the river they would travel north along the old dirt road on the east bank of the Shenandoah (now paved route 603). They would go to the present junction of routes 603 and 638 (Shenandoah Farms Grocery Store) and then continue up the mountain trail (now 638) to the Lehew pasture land on what is now the de Longfief home area adjacent to the border line of Blue Mountain.

Mrs. Jett said she remembers the departure of her grandfather and the cattle each Springtime and also the trip made in the Fall to bring the cattle back. However, she didn't make the trip herself until after her grandfather died. Capt. Lehew died December 3, 1918 at "Fairview." His wife, the former Sallie Machir Hopewell, had died earlier that year on February 19.

"After the death of my grandparents, our family lived at Fairview," Mrs. Jett said.

"As I remember, my father's health was poor. We didn't need the grazing land anymore, so my father and mother decided to sell it. But they made one last trip up there. It may have had something to do with the sale of the land."

She believes the trip would have been in the summer of 1919, the year after her grandparents died. The property was sold to Charles Haynie, a Howellsville farmer. Haynie sold the land to the de Longfiefs in 1956.

Mrs. Jett said she was probably ten years old when she made the trip to Blue Mountain with her parents.

"I know it was in August, because the peaches were ripe. The people were all peeling peaches when they arrived at the mountain," she said.

"Why I remember that so clearly," she said with a laugh, " was that the mountain people had told us there were no peaches up there. And when we got there, there were peaches all over the place. And there were lots of people there peeling peaches."

She remembers that she accompanied her father and mother on the trip.

"My mother had never been there before, either, so it was quite an adventure for us. We started out early in the morning in the horse and buggy. We packed a picnic lunch. I was sitting on the buggy seat between them. I remember that we took my favorite horse, Flora. I used to ride her around the farm," she said.

They followed the route the cattle used to take, across the river and then up the mountain road.

"When we got to the river we crossed at Morgan Ford. But it was still deep enough so that Flora had to swim across in the middle. And the water ran through the buggy so you would have to keep your feet up so they wouldn't get wet.

"We went up the road to the mountain. And, as I said, when we got there we surprised them all, as they were peeling the peaches. They had all the neighbors in, it seemed, to help them.

"We had our picnic up there and then we returned the same day."

She remembers seeing a house on the property.

"The house was small and a porch ran all along the front," she said.

Mrs. Jett's memory of the peaches could fit in with the Blue Mountain's distillery past. The Shiny Rock distillery had been located on the spot where the Lehew property was. Whether it was there in 1919 is not known. It is quite likely however that the furious activity Mrs. Jett witnessed ended up in peach brandy.

During several interesting hours of talking with Mrs. Jett, I was struck with how much the Civil War lives on in the mountains and valleys of old Virginia. She let me read the handwritten letters of her grandfather written from battlefields and Civil War place names throughout the South. I viewed the old photographs of this handsome Southern gentleman from the days when he was a young Captain of Infantry to his declining years as a distinguished-looking Virginian at "Fairview." As I talked to Mrs. Jett I thought of a book about the author of "Gone With the Wind" entitled "Margaret Mitchell of Atlanta." In it the author, Finis Farr, described how Margaret Mitchell grew up in Atlanta, surrounded by the memories of the war. Her companions, as a little girl, were the grizzled old veterans of that war, continually reliving the epic battles on park benches, all over Atlanta, as Margaret Mitchell sat fascinated, listening to every word.

This was how Mrs. Jett grew up in the Shenandoah Valley, surrounded by the actual scenes of the war, and, more important, an eager listener to the stories from the actual participants.

The Lehew family from which Capt. Lehew descends goes back to the very beginning of the nearby community of Front Royal. In fact, Front Royal, because of its founders, was once called Lehewtown. Peter Lehew, the great, great grandfather of Captain Lehew, purchased 200 acres "Lying on both sides of Greate Happy Creeke," in 1754. Portions of this land became what is now Front Royal.

Capt. Lehew's father Eli Lehew married a Miss Millar. They went to live on property she had inherited which was in the Lost River area of West Virginia.

Mrs. Jett recalls that "Capt. Lehew's mother died when he was quite small. His father remarried. His father died a year after the second marriage. His second wife, the former Sally Bronson of Winchester, sold the Lost River property and the family returned to Front Royal."

Capt. Lehew was born in Lost River, W. Va., on February 25, 1837. He was the youngest of four children (two brothers and a sister), all born in Werst Virginia. When the family returned to Front Royal, "the three eldest children remained with their stepmother. However, my grandfather went to live with his guardian, Capt. Samuel Gardiner," Mrs. Jett said.

The house where Captain Lehew grew up is called "Mountain Home" and still stands today on the east side of route 522 in Warren County near Chester Gap.

Mrs. Jett recalls there was a deep affection between the young Francis Lehew and his guardian Captain Gardiner.

"Captain Gardiner was a farmer and a slave owner. He had two daughters, but he had lost a son. There is a building in the yard at "Mountain Home," to the north of the house. This was a school building for Captain Gardiner's daughters. Captain Lehew's room was over that schoolhouse," Mrs. Jett said.

"Captain Lehew was like a brother to the Gardiner girls. When the younger one of them was born he rode the mule to Front Royal to get the doctor."

At the outbreak of the Civil War, Francis Lehew was 24 years old. Mrs. Jett said that he "had no formal military training. But he did belong to one of those militia companies in Front Royal."

"When his company left for Alexandria where they were joined with the 17th Virginia Infantry Regiment, he was the color bearer. The ladies of Front Royal had made a very handsome flag and had presented it to the company.

"At that time companies used to elect their officers. But that didn't work out. The person who might be very popular with the soldiers. That custom was abandoned later on.

"However, he was elected lieutenant in either 1861 or 1862. The Captain of the company was Robert Simpson. He was later promoted to Colonel on the battlefield. When he was promoted my grandfather was promoted to Captain."

Captain Lehew was in Gen. James Longstreet's command and saw action at Bull Run, Antietam and other areas wherever Longstreet's command went.

"He didn't go to Gettysburg. General (Robert E.) Lee was concerned about the bridges being burned in Virginia. His company and others were detached to guard bridges."

On September 17, 1862, Captain Lehew was wounded at Antietam Creek. That day the giants of the war – Gen. George McClellan of the Union Army and General Lee and Gen. Stonewall Jackson met in a battle that was considered the bloodiest of the war.

Bruce Catton, Civil War historian, wrote of the battle:

"Tactically, the battle was a draw. The Federals attacked savagely all day long, forcing the Confederates to give ground but never quite compelling the army to retreat, and when Lee's battered army held its position next day, McClellan did not renew the attack. But on the night of September 18 Lee took his worn-out army back to Virginia." [The American Heritage Picture History of the Civil War.]

Captain Lehew was among those wounded Confederate soldiers making their way back to Virginia.

"He was brought back by wagon to Winchester. The musket ball was still in his shoulder," Mrs. Jett said.

"He had to keep moving to avoid capture. After stopping at Winchester he moved farther south to 'Fairview' where his sister lived.

Thomas B. McKay, the descendant of one of the pioneer family's of the Valley had married Captain Lehew's sister. They lived at "Fairview."

"Then he went to Captain Gardiner, and then further down to Greene County, Virginia, with the musket ball still in his shoulder.

"When he was in Greene County he was treated for his wounds by an old colored woman, a slave. He offered her a silver dollar if she would get it out. She got the slug out.

"But he was seriously wounded and had lost a lot of blood. He was out of action for six to eight months.

"He was never wounded again. But he was captured at one of the closing battles of the war, at Five Forks, near Richmond. He spent the last weeks of the war at an officers prison camp on Johnson Island, Lake Erie."

Growing up in the Valley Mrs. Jett heard old timers recall how the war swirled around Front Royal, Winchester and in between.

The first battle of Gen. Jackson's Valley campaign began at Front Royal on May 23, 1862 and "ended near 'Fairview,'" Mrs. Jett said.

"It was a grim time in the Valley," she said. "The barns were burned. Practically every house along here was used as a hospital."

She remembers, when she was a little girl, seeing the blood stains on the parlor floor at "Fairview."

A great many were wounded in this area and 'Fairview' was one of the houses where they cared for soldiers. It was an old house at the time of the war. The floor was not too level. So the blood from the wounds would collect in a pool in the center of the floor.

"For years to come, even when I was a child, you could see this large stain in the floor when you would take up the carpet in the winter. Later the floors were stained so you don't see it anymore."

She remembers one story told about Uncle Ben, the McKay's slave at "Fairview," that took place during the battle of Front Royal.

"The Union soldiers were retreating north along the road from Front Royal. Just before that Uncle Ben had gone north from the house to mend a fence. The battle entrapped him. One Union soldier grabbed Uncle Ben, held him in front of him and used him as a shield. It scared him half to death. And when he broke loose from him Uncle Ben ran to the kitchen in the old log house. He went up the chimney and hid there."

Mrs. Jett said that her grandfather married shortly after the War ended. Francis Lehew married the former Sallie Macher Hopewell at Wardensville, Hardy County, West Virigina on May 26, 1868.

"They came back to Captain Gardiner's and lived in a small house, 'Meadow Cottage' just north of where Captain Gardiner lived," she said.

Mrs. Jett's mother, their first child, was born in "Meadow Cottage" on February 5, 1869.

Tragedy struck the family that same year. Mrs. McKay (Captain Lehew's sister) left "Fairview" in February in happy anticipation of seeing her new niece (Mrs. Jett's mother). The bridges that had been burned in the Civil War had not been rebuilt over the Shenandoah. She left "Fairview" on her horse, forded the river, but got quite wet during the crossing. She reached "Meadow Cottage" but came down with pneumonia and later died there.

Captain Lehew, three years later, in 1872, bought "Fairview" from his brother-in-law Thomas B. McKay.

The "Fairview" property, like much of the property in the Valley, descends from Lord Fairfax. The house was originally built in 1830 by the Grubb family. Captain Lehew built on the frame part of the house. Mrs. Jett sold "Fairview" several years ago. She lives a short distance away. Her present house also faces east, across the Valley, toward Blue Mountain.

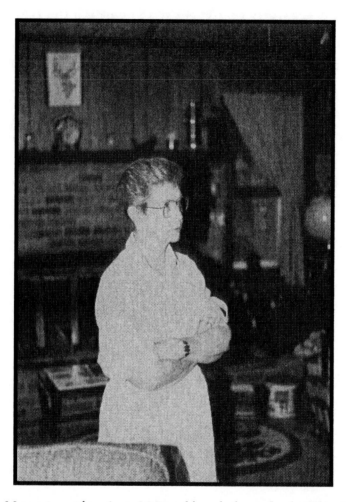

Blue Mountain resident Agnes McDonald made drapes for the White House and other famous Washington houses from her home on the mountain.

- 9 -
AGNES MCDONALD -BIRDS AND A BEAR

"There are seven widows up on that mountain."
– Charlie Reynolds

"We are thinking of calling this widow's peak."
– Agnes McDonald

Agnes McDonald of Chipmunk Trail is in touch with Shirley Temple and also the White House.

The diminutive Blue Mountain permanent resident makes draperies in the first floor workroom of her home. The draperies are of such good quality that several of them have found their way into the offices and homes of the famous.

"One day I got a call for a real rush job for the White House," she said.

The story was that the late President Lyndon Johnson was so upset with the draperies in the White House press room that "he wanted them changed immediately."

"He was going to Camp David for the weekend and said that he wanted the new draperies up when he returned," she said.

The material was rushed to her from Silver Spring, Maryland. The new draperies were made at Blue Mountain and returned to Washington in time to be hung at the White House for the President's Monday morning inspection.

Things are not always that dramatic on Chipmunk Trail. But Mrs. McDonald's draperies also hung in the African office of former Ambassador to Ghana, Shirley Temple Black and the office of the former Secretary of State Henry Kissinger and other prominent locations.

Formerly of Riverdale, Maryland, she is one of the several widows currently residing year-round at Blue Mountain.

"We are thinking of calling this widow's peak," she said with a smile.

She and her late husband, Charles McDonald, first came to Blue Mountain in the early 1960's.

Like many people who eventually decide to come to Blue Mountain, the McDonalds had close friends who owned property on the mountain.

"The Browers, our next door neighbors, had bought a place up here," she said. (Bernard and Virginia Brower built one of the early cabins on Far View Lane.)

She remembered their first visit was in the early 60's.

"We came up to visit the Browers on a Sunday. As I remember I didn't like Blue Mountain at first. Maybe it has got something to do with trees. The Browers lived farther down on the mountain and they were surrounded with a lot of pine trees. I don't like pines.

"Then one day," she related, "on another visit I took a walk up into this area to visit the Wilsons on Shady Lane. Bob Wilson is Virginia's brother.

"Well, I really liked it up here. It was the first time I had seen these big tulip trees. I fell in love with these trees," she said gesturing toward the tulip poplars in front of her house.

From then on, she recalls, the idea of coming to Blue Mountain consumed her.

"But my husband didn't like the idea. I remember being in the hospital and having a lot of time to think and I started to think about how we could live up here. When I got out of the hospital I said: 'Maybe we could refinance our mortgage.' He didn't go for it. But I am persistent when I get my mind set on something."

Eventually the McDonalds decided to build a second home at Blue Mountain. The shell of their present house was put up by Blue Mountain Construction Co. in 1965.

The McDonalds had three young daughters and the whole family pitched in to clear the lot. The daughters are Susan, Kathy and Lorraine.

Lorraine (now Mrs. Daniel McCallister), the youngest of the three, didn't like Blue Mountain either when she first came here. She was 13 then.

"Blue Mountain meant poison ivy to me," she recalls.

"We used to come up to clear the lot and I used to get poison ivy real bad. Mother bought all of us girls gloves to wear. I remember sitting on a log and covering my face with the gloves. I was so sad.

"I remember one day the car broke down and we had to go to Front Royal to get help. And I thought, 'My gosh, Front Royal is so big.' Now I don't think it is big at all."

Lorraine and Danny McCallister and their seven-year-old son, Charley, rented a house on Trillium Trail and lived year-round on the mountain in 1975 and 1976. This past year they lived with Agnes McDonald , and four dogs and four cats on Chipmunk Trail.

In 1966, the year after the McDonalds built their house, Charles McDonald died of a heart attack. The following years Agnes McDonald brought up her three daughters by herself. Along with help from her father and other friends the Blue Mountain house was finished on weekends.

"As the girls grew up and got married or were ready to take care of themselves, I kept thinking about living at Blue Mountain.

"I would tell the girls: 'I'm going up to the mountains' and they would get all excited and say 'You can't go up there by yourself! What if something happens to you?'"

Eventually the persistent Agnes McDonald won out. She has been a permanent resident of Blue Mountain since July 1, 1971. Most of the time she has lived by herself. How is it living alone on a mountain?

"I don't mind it. I like it. We have a community here, too. It's not all that lonely. I like this natural way of life – with the trees and the birds and the animals. It grows on you."

But even the hardy Agnes wasn't all that calm one Fall evening in 1975. That was the night of "the bear."

"Over the years I have put out food for the raccoons. This was an evening in the Fall. I had put out the food. It is fun to watch them, especially when the baby raccoons come along, too.

"They didn't come for awhile so I went downstairs to watch the news on TV. Then I heard all of this commotion out there. I said to myself 'my golly there must be a dozen raccoons out there – because they bring their babies sometimes."

I came up to look and the food was gone. Well, raccoons don't eat that fast. And then (she pointed) I had a peanut butter log right there and it was swinging."

(She would cut slits in a log, put peanut butter in, and hang it up for the birds.)

"I said, gee, that log is swinging, but it's not windy. Why, I thought, is that log swinging. Then I saw this paw go swiping past. I saw that it was a black bear. He was hard to see, at first, because he is black and it was dark.

"He was sitting on the railing and hitting the peanut butter log. He finally knocked it down. I thought he was going to break the glass to the outside porch door. I ran in and called Lee Lipsomb. We had heard rumors that there was a bear on the mountain.

"'She said:' 'Who is it?'

"I said, 'It's Agnes.'

"She said, 'You don't sound like yourself.'

"I said, 'Well, there's a bear on the porch.'

Mrs. Lipscomb said she would call some neighbors and they would come down.

"So," Mrs. McDonald said, "I just kept my eye on the bear while I waited for them

"The bear knocked the peanut butter log down and licked out all the peanut butter.

"I had some suet in the bird feeder, which was up on a pole on the porch. He could smell that. The next thing I knew he was trying to get the suet. So he climbed up on the dogwood tree but the tree bent over so he decided that wasn't the way to do it.

"He went down and climbed up on top of my car and got bear prints all over my car. I wouldn't let anyone wash the window for awhile. Everyone wanted to see the bear prints.

"Finally he came back up on the steps and put his mouth on the pole support and shook and shook until it came down.

"I had another peanut butter log out in the yard. He domlished that. He really made a mess out there.

"Then he came back on the porch and he stood up at the door and his nose came to the top panel. I thought he was going to push the door in. I hollered loud and I guess that scared him and he left.

"The bear returned, however, every night for a week.

"I put the food farther out. He was very interesting to watch. He didn't bother anything after that. He would come in the early evening, eat the food and leave."

The bear was eventually shot and killed.

"I was down at the post office one day and someone asked if I heard about the bear. They said it was shot by some one at Skyland Estates." (a nearby development).

Mrs. McDonald said she was saddened when she heard the bear was shot.

"I called the warden the day after the first bear came. He said if the bear became a nuisance he would come and get it. But otherwise he though the bear would be shot during the hunting season. I don't believe they should shoot them, tho. He didn't harm anything."

Mrs. McDonald said the bear had metal clips in his ears. This is the way Virginia conservation officials keep track of the bear population. It was estimated that there were 1,600 bears in the Blue Ridge Mountains of Virginia in the census of 1970. When a bear leaves the public parkland and becomes what is considered a "nuisance" the conservation officials capture the bear by using a tanquilizer gun and return him to the parklands. "Nuisance" bears in the Front Royal area are usually returned to the Shenandoah National Forest. The Skyline Drive Goes through the forest and visitors to the area often see bears in that area.

Mrs. McDonald's kindness to animals, especially the feathered variety, may have attracted a wide variety of birds to Blue Mountain.

"I don't remember too many birds up here, at least in this part of the mountain, before we came here," she said.

Her peanut logs and bird feeders provide a welcome resting place.

"The first bird to come was a cardinal," she said.

As the months and years passed many more came. Regular visitors now include cardinals, blue jays, chickadees, flickers ("they jabber to each other all the time"), tit mice, nut hatches, evening grosbeaks ("they eat everything"), gold finches, woodpeckers, (several kinds: piliated, downy, hairy and red belly) and even flying squirrels ("they are the size of chipmunks").

Every now and then, she said, a sad-eyed owl will come and sit on the railing.

"No, it's not lonesome up here," she said with a smile, as a chicadee flew by her glassed-in porch.

"And every Spring now, for the past few years, a pair of morning doves arrive right on schedule."

Agnes McDonald (no relation to the McDonald family that use to lumber the mountain) has her hands full these days. She is the president of the Blue Mountain Property Owners Association. This is an organization that is concerned about keeping the mountain as beautiful and peaceful as the early days when the general area of Front Royal and Winchester was not as populous and bustling as it is today.

Blue Mountaineers are convinced that progress doesn't always mean that the quality of life gets any better. The organization wants to have improved roads and living conditions. But too much progress isn't wanted. A case in point is the proliferation of towers on top of adjacent Blue Mountain land. Agnes McDonald and other Blue Mountaineers keep leading the protest against any more towers. But they haven't been too successful.

The beauty of Blue Mountain is that it is high above the surrounding Shenandoah Valley.

"We'd like to keep it this way. We just don't need any more towers up here," McDonald said.

- 10 -
Freezeland –
The Great Orchard

About two miles up from Linden, the winding road to Blue Mountain passes an apple orchard. The casual visitors see a few apple trees and they probably presume they are on the fringe of a small orchard.

Many are surprised to find that Freezeland Orchard is an enormous size -- more than 800 acres (comparable to the size of Blue Mountain) and containing more than 20,000 apple trees. It also has a fascinating history dating back to the turn of the century. It was an era that saw the beginning of many of the great Virginia apple orchards. The orchard also has an international flavor. Before World War I most of its apples were purchased by England. In the 1920s Argentina provided a big market for Freezeland apples.

Today the giant orchard is under the supervision of Ben Lacy III: a descendant of one of the original three families who founded Freezeland in 1906.

Lacy is an engaging person whose interests encompass a wide and expert knowledge of fruit growing blended with a love of the history of the Freezeland and Blue Mountain area.

"As a boy I rode my pony on these old mountain roads. Many of them were just logging trails, then. It was a great place to come to on summer vacations when I was a youngster," Lacy said. Ben Lacy was born in 1922 and is actually the third generation connected with the long history of Freezeland.

Lacy has the old deed to Freezeland. It reads:

"This deed was made 20 February, 1906 between Richard H. Dulaney, widower and C. Gratton Crawford, Frank B. Crawford and William Mac C. White….. being the tract of the land knows as Friezeland….."

"Being the same land conveyed to said Richard H. Dulaney by William T.W. Taliferro and his wife by deed dated October 28, 1858 and recorded in Fauquier County deed book 57 on page 400."

The old deed, Lacy said, is interesting for several reasons. He noted that the old spelling for Freezeland was "Friezeland."

"I was told this old spelling relates to the beautiful views of the Shenandoah Valley that you receive from this mountain – like a frieze – and that is why the mountain received this early name.

"Over the years the local people changed the spelling to Freezeland," he said.

[In my own research I have never found one general name for this mountain between Manassas Gap (Linden) and Ashby Gap (Paris). Some early geological survey maps call the mountain "Freezeland."

Many people refer to it as "Paris Mountain." In recent conversations with various people in Front Royal, I was surprised to hear them casually refer to the whole mountain as "Blue Mountain." Because "Blue Mountain" does comprise large acreage on the very top of the mountain, and it is a community of people, there is likelihood that as years go by this will become the accepted name for the mountain.]

Another interesting aspect of the old deed, Lacy said, was the appearance of the Dulaney and Taliaferro names. Both of these families are related, Lacy said, to the Marshall Family. As has been pointed out earlier, all of these mountain lands, in this part of Virginia descend from a great English land grant to Lord Fairfax. After the Revolutionary War, much of the same land, including Blue Mountain and Freezeland passed through litigation to the family of John Marshall, the Chief Justice of the Supreme Court.

Mrs. Elizabeth Engle of Winchester, daughter of Frank J. Crawford, one of the original founders of Freezeland, described how the orchard began:

"My father, Frank Crawford and his brother Gratton Crawford were born and grew up at Kernstown, near Winchester. Both of them had gone to Washington and Lee to college. They had a childhood friend, William White.

"As the years passed the three men kept in contact with each other. Dr. White became a Presbyterian minister, pastor of The First Presbyterian Church in Raleigh, North Carolina. My father was teaching at McDonough School for Boys, outside of Baltimore.

"Uncle Gratton was a farmer at the old homestead, Hilandale, near Kernstown," she said.

[Hilandale is a beautiful, historic home south of Winchester – rich in the history of Colonial American and Civil War days.]

"Uncle Gratton, for a long time, had this idea of beginning an apple orchard. He was looking for a piece of mountain property as it was known that apples grow well in mountain areas. When he finally found Freezeland, he contacted my father and Dr. White. They put in $5,000 each and bought the first acreage – for $15,000 – six hundred acres of mountain land. This is how Freezeland Orchard began.

"Uncle Gratton, because of his knowledge of farming, began the orchard. He dug the holes, he put in the first trees. Many times he would ride over from Kernstown on his horse. Other times he would come over by train, to surpervise and work at the young orchard."

Ben Lacy, who is the grandson of Dr. William White, is the principal owner and stockholder of Freezeland today. It remains a family business with the remainder of the stock owned by the descendants of the three original families.

Lacy explained that Freezeland was begun during an expansion period for orchards.

"They were looking for hilly or mountainous land where you get a weather break, where the westerly and easterly winds meet. This is the type of land that is good for growing apples. You get a weather break up in Pennsylvania, along the ridges of the mountain. So when they found this land they knew it should be good for growing apples."

Col. Dulaney, the former owner of the Freezeland preoperty, was a wealthy landowner from Upperville, Virginia. He was the founder and president of the Upperville Horse Show for more than 50 years. This horse show, held every year in June, advertises itself as the "oldest horse show in America."

During Col. Dulaney's ownership of Freezeland, (from 1858 to 1906) there was a substantial dairy farm on the property.

Lacy has an avid interest in the history of the area. (He received an A.B. in history from Davidson College). He said when the Crawford-White families purchased Freezeland there was an "ancient, three-story barn on the property." (The barn was later torn down.)

"When we tore down some of barns we found pieces of money that had dates in the 1830s and 1850s on it. The oldest building still standing is the oldstone spring house, just as you come in the entrance on the right. We estimate that was built in the 1850s.

"Right above it is the old Cooper shop, where barrels and crates were made. That used to be a slave quarters. We found old money in there, too," Lacy said.

In the old days of the dairy farm, Lacy said, the farmers would take the milk down the old road to the railroad siding at Linden in two-wheel carts. They would place the milk in the Springhouse there and separate the cream from the milk.

"They would then ship the cream into Washington by train. The roads weren't very good in those days, so the railroads played an important role," he said.

Apple growing was a profitable business at the turn of the century. Strangely enough the big money was not being made in America but in England.

"The English loved American apples," Lacy said.

"They would pay twenty-three dollars a barrel on the docks of Liverpool, England. That was a fabulous price in those days."

Thus, the first of hundreds of thousands of Freezeland apples were consumed in Great Britain. It could be said that many of the great Virginia and New York State orchards were begun because of the high-priced English market.

Lacy said that the English liked small, tasty apples, a little on the tart side. Some of the names of there apples (many of them no longer produced) were: King David, Bascum, Jonathan and Grimes Golden.

They were an early ripening apple. They would pick them early, pack them in barrels and ship them to England, arriving in England before the English crop was ready to be picked.

This profitable English market lasted until just after World War I.

"About that time," Lacy said, "America put a tariff on the English steel and woolen goods. England retaliated by putting a tariff on American agricultural products coming into England. So, the market was killed. We couldn't ship any more apples to England under those conditions. It was too expensive for us. I remember my grandfather recalling that this was a very serious time for the Freezeland orchard and for many orchards in Virginia. We thought we were sunk."

However, another development, also of an international nature, happened shortly afterwards.

"Luckily, America had a good trade agreement with Argentina. They had been shipping us beef for many years. Now, it was learned that the Argentinians liked American apples," Lacy said.

Thus, in the 1920s and the 1930s Freezeland enjoyed another resurgence and many of its apples went to Argentina.

"We had been growing an apple called the Gano, a kin to the Ben Davis," Lacy said.

"This is a very large, red apple that the Argentinians liked. So the Gano saved us."

Another crisis occurred, Lacy said, when Argentina found it could develop its own apple orchards on the fertile land along the Rio Negro River.

"That shut us out again. It made us take another hard look at our operation," Lacy said.

Since World War II many of the Eastern apple orchards, like Freezeland, have been saved by the fruit processing industry.

"Most of our apples are now sold to fruit processing plants to make canned apples, apple sauce and apple slices. We still grow a variety of apples but our main apple is the York Imperial. This is a very fine slicing apple," Lacy said.

The switch to selling to processors transformed the Freezeland Orchard. There are now only a few trees left of the original plantings in 1906. Apple growing is a long, slow process. It takes fifteen years, Lacy estimates "before you actually get anything off a tree.

"You have to plan ahead for a long time and you don't know if you are actually going to hit the market with an apple that people like," he said.

"Right now (1977) I just can't get anyone to pick apples," Lacy said.

"And the U.S. Department of Labor has restrictions against imported labor. For the last seven years I have had to get men from Jamaica to come in to pick the apples. They are hard workers and they love to come in. After they pick apples here they go to Florida to cut sugar cane. They make enough money in a few months to support themselves in Jamaica for the rest of the year."

Although there was high employment in the summer of 1977, few young Americans were attracted to the comparatively low-paying job of apple-picking. Foreign workers, on the other hand, are attracted to the jobs. Apple pickers in Virginia, in 1977, were paid the minimum wage of %2.65 an hour with ambitious piece-workers able to make four dollars an hour.

The severe drought of 1977, the worst in 30 years, also was a problem for Lacy. Looking out over the orchard he said:

"The nectarines are the size of golf balls. They should be the size of tennis balls by now," he said.

Freezeland orchard has an immediate outlet for its apples. Lacy owns the Apple House, a nearby fruit and grocery store on Route 55, near Linden.

Many Blue Mountaineers, however, prefer to go right to the source, the Freezeland orchard itself, to purchase their apples. And, in doing, they keep in contact with a part of their own history.

He pointed to an old dusty book on the top shelf. It was entitled: "The Apples of New York."

"Those books," he said, "are the best, and most expensive books ever written on apples. New York State has a tremendous variety of apples."

Lacy has an interesting mixture of forces in his background. Both his grandfather (Dr. White) and his father, Dr. Ben Lacy Jr. (92 years old in 1977) were Presbyterian ministers. He grew to love history. It was his major subject in his college days. He was with the Marine Corps in World War II and rose to the rank of Captain. After the war he took his Master's degree in pomology (the science and practice of fruit growing) at Virginia Polytechnic Institute. After graduation he managed an orchard at Boone's Mill, Franklin County, Virginia. Since 1951, he has been at Freezeland, most of the time in the role of supervisor and principal owner.

"When I came to Freezeland in 1951, Dr. Frank Cawford was in charge of the orchard," Lacy said.

[Dr. Crawford, son of Grattan Crawford was a medical doctor and a Presbyterian medical missionary to China. After being forced out of China in 1915 because of the onset of World War I, he returned to America.]

"I had a tremendous admiration for him. He was like a father to me. He taught me a great deal about how to manage an orchard," Lacy said.

At this current writing the Eastern apple industry in beset by serious labor problems.

- 11 -
1906 – The First Summer Visitors

The year is 1906. It is a lazy Victorian summer. It is also the year that the Blue Mountain area saw its first summer visitors.

When the Crawford and White families founded Freezeland Orchard in 1906, they started a business. But they also began something else. They started a tradition. In 1906 the mountain, for the first time, became a "summer place."

"Father and mother wanted us to have a little of that life. That is a page of history in our life – for the three of us. It is entirely different from anything else we ever did."

The speaker is Mrs. Eleanor Crawford Jackson, the former Eleanor Crawford, daughter of C. Grattan Crawford, one of the founders of Freezeland. Mrs. Jackson, who was born in 1887, lives with her sister Louisa Crawford, born in 1894, at Hilandale, the historic Crawford family home at Kernstown, near Winchester, Virginia.

In 1906 Eleanor, then 19, and Louisa, then 12, were among 17 Crawford young people, relatives and friends who spent the first summer vacation at the mountain.

In July of 1977 I spent a memorable evening at Hilandale talking with Eleanor and Louisa about this first, and subsequent, vacations. Also present was their cousin Mrs. Elizabeth Engle, the daughter of Frank Crawford, another Freezeland founder. Mrs. Engle, born in 1910, told of her first impressions of the mountain when she first vacationed there in 1919.

Louisa remembers that first summer on the mountain:

"We went over on the train from Kernstown. We stopped at Strasburg to change trains. We waited for hours in Strasburg for the train to Linden."

(The Baltimore and Ohio Railroad ran from Kernstown to Strasburg. The Southern Railroad ran from Strasburg to Linden.)

"The Reason we took the train is that mother had to take all the supplies and the food and the bedding. At Linden you could probably get some flour and sugar. But when we got up on the mountain we were seven miles from Front Royal. So we had to take everything with us."

When they reached Linden they waited for the horses and buggies to come down from Freezeland to take them up the mountain.

"It was an exciting time going up that mountain not knowing where we were going. It was like a great adventure. Imagine," Louisa's eyes sparkled as she recalled the 71-year old memory, "seventeen of us going up that mountain for the first time."

That first year and for the first several summers they lived in tents and slept on the ground. But that first summer vacation was marred by rain.

"We all lived in these four tents that we brought with us," Louisa said.

"It rained every day, except one, for three weeks. You could put your hand out and feel the water running down the mountain.

"But no one took any cold and every one had ravenous appetites. How mother and father ever got enough for us to eat, I have yet to find out."

In future summers, however, the weather was better, and even more friends and relatives came.

"When Dr. (William) White built his house there in 1907 his family used to come up from North Carolina and we had an even larger crowd.

"We would all gather around the campfire by the tents every night and sing songs and toast marshmallows," Louisa said.

The mountain atmosphere even inspired some poetry. The following excerpt of a longer poem was written by Willie Marshall, a young friend of the Crawfords, from Winchester, circa 1906:

"Beneath the group of chestnut trees as if by nature made, A rustic table thrice a day with dainties rare is gaily spread. And here about the festive board when the horn of plenty calls, The jovial folks assemble to drink the health of each and all.

After an evening just at twilight a fire roars upward high, From out a pile of skeletons of ye old and fierce Bo-Ji. And around this campfire gleaming sit the party in a ring. For until the stars grow sleepy you can hear them play and sing. All this the moon will tell for there is more if you will win. To echo yell aloud – Yahoo – He will answer: "Dew, Drop In."

Refrain:

O the mountains, O the mountains where the air is fresh and firm. Where the sparkling rills go leaping, to shade and shine."

Mrs. Engle pointed out two interesting aspects of the poem. There were chestnut trees on the mountain in the early days of Freezeland. However, as years went by the trees were destroyed by the blight that destroyed chestnut trees throughout the Blue Ridge in the early 1900s.

Also, the use of the term "Beaugye" intrigues Mrs. Engle.

"I think it was a 'made-up' name by the children who came up here those first summers. In the poem it seems to refer to ghosts of Indian warriors, or something like that. But there was also a place where we used to walk and, which is now part of Skyland Estates, where you get a spectacular view of the valley. This place was also called "Bo-Ji."

Louisa Crawford remembers that the second year, in 1907, when they went up, the tenant houses had been built for the regular employees of the orchard.

"Father reserved two rooms in one of the houses. Mother and father stayed in those rooms the second year. But we had the tents for a number of years," she said.

She remembers her father planting the first apple trees.

"Father held every tree that was to be planted in his hands." The first orchard was back of the old 3-story barn (now torn down) and up on top of the mountain.

There were romances on the mountain.

Eleanor Crawford was nineteen when she went to the mountain that first time in 1906. One of the guests was John Long Jackson of Baltimore.

"We had a nice picture of John and Eleanor. They were up on the mountain gazing into the distance. We always said that they were looking into the furture," Louisa said with a smile. Four years later Eleanor and John were married.

John Jackson went on to become an Episcopal priest. In his later years he was the Episcopal Bishop of Louisiana.

Ben Lacy also recalled:

"My father courted my mother up on the mountain, during summer vacations."

Louisa remembered that Freezeland lived up to its name, in those days, when it came to take a bath.

"We had a bathhouse," she said, "in back of the White cottage. The stream ran back there. We put an old tub there. Well, that was the coldest water! They were the coldest baths I ever had," she said with a laugh.

"It was a very crude, but those were happy days," Eleanor said.

The Crawford sisters remember that their beautiful old Kernstown home, Hilandale, was also the center of activity in their younger days.

"This old house," Louisa said, "Was bursting with people. My sister and my brother Frank (later a medical missionary to China) had all of their parties here. All of our friends came."

When summer came, many of the friends who had come to Hilandale were guests at the mountain, too.

On a clear day, from the rear veranda of Hilandale, you can look across lush green fields and, off in the distance, see the towers on Blue Mountain, nestled in the Blue Ridge.

On the evening I was there Louisa Crawford had given me a special tour of the old house, with emphasis on its role in the Civil War.

Looking out from the verandah, towards Blue Mountain as though she was lost in memory, for a moment, she said:

"There were 30,000 of them."

"Thirty-thousand?" I asked, mystified by what she meant.

"Yankees. Thirty thousand Yankees were out in that field."

As the war moved into its final months, Northern troops massed in the Winchester and Kernstown area, preparing for the final drive through the Shenandoah Valley. The soldiers camped for several days on the Hilandale estate.

Louisa remembered a happier time at Hilandale, too.

"Some years, in the Spring, father would go off from here on horseback, to the orchard on the mountain.

"Sometimes he would take cattle over from here to graze on the mountain. He would take them through the old country roads until he got to the sunken bridge (Morgans Ford) over the (Shenandoah) river. Then he would go on the road to Howellsville and up the mountain that way. Other times he would go through the Dismal Hollow area (now route 647) and go up that way.

"In the Springtime, when father would come back from the mountain he would bring mother some trilliums and wild geraniums and ferns," she said. "We still have some of them in our rockery."

Louisa, today, has a pungent reminder of those early days on the mountains.

"In those days, sleeping in the tents on the mountain, when the mosquitoes would bother us we would pick some pennyroyal. We would put the pennyroyal under our pillows, before we went to sleep, and the mosquitoes wouldn't bother us."

Pennyroyal is a small, green plant related to mint with a sharp scent. She has planted pennyroyal, from the mountain, in her front lawn garden.

"As soon as I pick the pennyroyal, I am back at Freezeland again," she said.

Mrs. Engle, the only child of Mr. and Mrs. Frank Crawford, represents another generation of "summer visitors" to the mountain. She made her first visit there in 1919 when she was nine years old.

"We used to come by train, too, from Winchester to Strasburg to Linden. Only, by then we were coming for the whole summer, for three months.

"When we got to Linden we would be met by someone on horseback and a horse and buggy for my mother and me to ride in. There was also a four-mule team pulling a wagon. We put all of our trunks and supplies in there.

"Everybody in those days went to the mountains, to a place like this, or the Spa down at Seven Fountain in Fort Valley, or Passage Creek or Berkeley Springs."

She remembers the old stone spring house (which is still standing) was in actual use in those days.

"There were always plenty of springs at Freezeland, plenty of cold water. We kept all of our food in the spring house – milk and vegetables – to keep it cold. We were always carrying things back and forth to the spring house. We picked cherries and black berries and canned them."

Mrs. Engle now owns "Tree Top," a summer cottage that was begun by her father in 1919 and finished in 1920. "Tree Top" is on the south side of Route 638, across from the main orchard complex.

"The first house built for summer visitors was the house next to this one. That was built by Dr. William White in 1907. Uncle Grattan Cawford built a house for his family in 1916 – across the road from "Tree Top" – that was called "Seldom Inn."

She remembers when they would bring a horse over for her to ride in the summer – from Winchester – they would ride the horse down what is now Route 522 to Double Tollgate, then to White Post, across the river at Morgans Ford, to Howellsville and up the mountain that way.

"My father and mother let me have a horse but they didn't let me go very far. They said there were too many moonshiners around. Also, they were always afraid that I would get lost," she recalled.

[As related in an earlier chapter the Blue Mountain area, from the early 1900s on, was a favorite place for moonshiners, who made illegal whiskey commonly known as "white lightning." Also, there were two legal distilleries on the mountain near the Howellsville side.]

The early roads up the mountain were crude and rocky. They were corduroy roads, roads made by lying logs, side by side. They also had "Thank you ma'ms," the expression used for small ditches that were dug in the roads at various intervals. These were made so that horses, tired from dragging heavy loads of logs or lumber, could rest by letting the back wheels of the wagon lock in the ditches. Mrs. Engle remembers that "one of the most exciting times, was when Mr. McDonald would come by hauling his lumber, with those big horses pulling the wagons."

She remembers the Freezeland used fine huge Percheron horses for its work and she believes that McDonald used Percherons, too.

[Jim McDonald, the lumberman, lumbered the entire Blue Mountain area from 1915 on. He and his wife and eleven children lived a short distance from the present Blue Mountain Information Office.]

"The McDonalds," she said, "would cut logs and lumber the logs back in the forest. Then they would haul them down by horse and wagon to Linden, where they loaded it all on railroad freight cars.

"They cut the wood for the beginning of this house and I am sure for Uncle Grattan's house, too.

"One of the big things I can remember as a child was watching those teams go up and down the road and the way those teams, with their heavy, heavy loads would use the 'thank you am'ams' as they would go by. And they would be slapping the horses as they would go down the roads.

"The McDonalds were big men. I didn't know the McDonalds by name because I was a child.

"I think of them as the first mountain men that I would have known. And they always came out of nowhere and went back to nowhere. They just disappeared out in that direction," she said pointing toward Blue Mountain.

She also remembers the old blacksmith shop at Freezeland.

"It was located on this side (south side of 638) of the road, by the stream where the road begins to turn going toward Linden. The blacksmith shop was there and all of those horses and mules were shod there."

One of her vivid memories is of Dr. Ben Lacy, the father of Ben Lacy III, the present director of Freezeland. Dr. Lacy married Emma White, the daughter of Dr. William White, a founder of Freezeland.

"As I recall, Dr. Lacy, who had been a chaplain in World Was I, had just come up to Freezeland that summer for his vacation."

"One of the farm hands had found a horse bleeding to death. The artery had been severed apparently when the horse went against some farm machinery.

"Dr. Lacy put a tourniquet on the horse, stopped the bleeding and saved the horse's life. Everyone, as I recall, was deeply grateful for the quick action he took.

"Ordinarily, we would have called a veterinarian from the Remount Station in Front Royal. (U.S. Cavalry horses were trained at the station.) They would have gotten up here eventually. But by that time the horse would have died."

She recalls hat the roads, for years, were in very bad shape, rough and rocky. She believes that she witnessed the first car to come up the road from Linden. The road was so bad the car broke its axle. She read from her diary for Tuesday, August 24, 1920:

"The Phillips came to see us in their car, a Model T. They stuck in the mud. They broke the axle of their car. So they had to stay all night. Wednesday, the Phillips left."

The concern over the poor roads, Mrs. Engle said, took up much of her father's (Frank Crawford) free time, during their summer vacations.

"Every day, after the noon meal he would go out with surveying instruments trying to find some route with not too steep a grade. Also a route that would not be too expensive.

"When the CCCs (Civilian Conservation Corps) decided to build the present road (1933) it was a blessing to us," she said.

Mrs. Engle said that the men who worked on the road lived at the CCC barrack – like structure in what is known as Dismal Hollow. This is about two miles west of Linden on Route 647. It was later used as a chicken farm. Today the barrack is a vacant building.

"I was told that this was the first CCC camp in the United States," she said.

One of her more vivid memories of summer on the mountain was about escaped convicts.

"This was another reason why my parents didn't let me stray too far from home. There was a prison camp at Double Tollgate as there is today, about seven miles from the mountain. From time to time there were reports of escaped convicts. I don't recall anyone ever getting hurt but it did cause a lot of excitement for us.

One of the entries in her diary reads:

"Thursday, Mr. Teets was pruning in the orchard when he saw two colored men – one was half-Indian, the other was black. He phoned Front Royal. They said these were the convicts that got out of the camp.. We were all very much excited about them."

Mrs. Engle remembers that she spent her summer vacations at Freezeland from 1919 to 1926.

"When I was 16, it was the last summer I spent here in the early period. But we reopened the place in 1947 and my family and I have been coming here since then."

The Blue Mountain area was famous for its springtime trilliums and lady slippers long before there was an actual place called Blue Mountain.

Ben Lacy remembers that the late Governor and Senator Harry F. Byrd was very fond of the trilliums and he would be seen walking in the area where the present towers are.

"I believe," Lacy said, "that Blue Mountain area is the only place in Virginia where you get this much trillium. Senator Byrd once had a place to preserve all of it under something like a state park. But for some reason it never went through."

"I remember one year, without him knowing about it, the state trucks came up route 638 and put insect spray on the edge of the road. This killed some of the trillium.

"Oh, man, was Senator Byrd mad. He really laid them out. They never came back here and sprayed again," Lacy said with a laugh.

Mrs. Engle said the Blue Mountain trillium and lady slippers were so rare that busloads of people from Washington came in the 1946's in the springtime to the mountain to see them.

"In the 1960s the Orchid Society of Washington came and I used to love to join them. One of their members told me that this area has rare flowers and plants that are only seen in such abundance here. Some rare orchids were also found here on occasion."

In the long ago there were fierce mountain lions in the Blue Ridge Mountains. Mrs. Engle believes, however, that a mountain lion, or lions, was spotted in the Freezeland Orchard as recently as the mid-1960s.

"About ten years ago," she said, " some of the men working in the orchard came out of the bunkhouse where they lived, early in the morning. They went toward the packing house and they had to pass some tall grass. They said they saw a large cat like animal jump down off a tree limb and go bounding in the tall grass. It really scared them.

"Violet Smedley, the wife of Clyde Smedley, who was the foreman at Freezeland at the time, knew that her daughter in Front Royal had an encyclopedia and showed the pictures to the men. The men pointed to the picture of the mountain lion.

"People who should know, said there were no mountain lions in this area. Then, about that time, people over near Warrenton said they spotted a mountain lion.

"I began to read up on what they are like The books said a mountain lion has a terrible cry, like a woman screaming.

"Clyde Smedly said there was another time earlier, in this lifetime, when he had run across them. Once he had gone down the mountain on horseback to Linden to meet the train. He got about half way down when he heard this piercing scream. His horse nearly shook him off.

Smedley said the horse would not move for some time, because he was so scared.

"In the old days, when there really were mountain lions in the Blue Ridge, I was told, the horses were scared because the lions would jump from a tree right on top of them."

Mrs. Engle's husband, Dr. Raleigh Engle, a Presbyterian minister, died in 1969. She has two daughters- Elizabeth Engle Stoddard and Margaret Engle Trumbo.

Mrs. Engle still looks forward to her trips to Freezeland. The day I visited her at "Tree Top," the fourth generation that grew out of the Crawford line at Freezeland, her grandchildren, were enjoying themselves poring over the old pictures in the scrapbook.

"There are a lot of happy memories here, and a lot of good times right now, too," she said.

- 12 -
CHILDHOOD MEMORIES -
RIDING A PONY ON BLUE MOUNTAIN -
CIRCA 1930

Ben Lacy, owner-manager of Freezeland, the giant orchard next to Blue Mountain, is shown at the Apple House, where the latest product of the company, Alpenglow, a sparkling, non-alcoholic apple cider, is produced.

"When I was a boy I would ride my pony back in there, where Blue Mountain is today. There were a lot of old logging roads in there. It was fun going exploring. This mountain was a great place for a kid to come to in the summertime."

Ben Lacy is talking, in his soft Virginia drawl, about his childhood memories of the Blue Mountain and Freezeland areas. Lacy is the principal owner and manager of Freezeland Orchard today.

The world that Ben Lacy explored as a child was a fascinating one. It was peopled by lumbermen, moonshiners, Appalachian mountaineers, an old copper mine, Civil War outposts and an apple grower who created the "largest orchard in the world."

Lacy was born in 1922. He was a "summer visitor" to the White cottage when he was a year old. The cottage was built in 1907 by his grandfather Dr. William White, one of the founders of Freezeland Orchard. It stands today across the road from the main entrance to the orchard.

Lacy's happiest memories, however, were in the late 1920s and the early 1930s, when he was in his pre-teens.

"When I was a boy when we would come up here in the 1920s and 1930s, we would park our cars in Linden. My parents rented garages in Linden and put the cars there.

"They would meet us at Linden with a four-mile team. The women and the trunks would ride on the wagon. The men and the boys would walk behind. In our group would be my grandfather and grandmother, my mother and father and aunts and uncles and children."

"Some people would come up for a month and others would come and spend all summer. Some people liked the mountain, other people didn't like it. Aunt Tanney didn't like it, she said she saw too many snakes."

"My mother would come up for all summer. My father (Dr. Ben Lacy) who was a minister, would come up for a month."

Lacy's most providential experience was the fact that a Dr. Eliot, a friend of his family, used to raise Shetland ponies.

"Dr. Eliot," Lacy said, "used to live in that pretty house with the white columns on route 55, about a mile east of Linden.

"He had several Shetland ponies. He used to raise them. He didn't have enough pasture for them to graze on. In the summertime he would let the local people have a pony, if you would take care of them, ride them and feed them.

"We would always get our ponies there. When we would first come up at the beginning of the summer we would get four or five ponies, one for me and ponies for the other youngsters who were with us.

We would ride back in the mountains on the old logging trails and every where."

Lacy's childhood journeys took him to some interesting places in a Huck Finn type of world.

"There was an old road that went down to where the Blue Mountain tennis courts are now. We used to ride down that road on our ponies. Up from where the tennis courts are now, there used to be an old barrel factory. They used to make staves for whiskey barrels. It was quite a big operation. It was owned by the Borden Lumber Company. During the depression the old factory closed. During the depression a lot of the land up here was affected. The old factory ended up owned by the insurance companies."

Lacy said he thinks the barrel factory was there from around the turn of the century and that it collapsed financially in the 1920s.

"The money depression came in the early 1930s. But the agricultural depression came in the 1920s. All the farms business around here had borrowed from the insurance companies. Then the agricultural depression came and the land went to the insurance companies. Then in the 30s the insurance companies lost all of their money in the stock market."

"We used to ride down there and play around the old factory. There were poeople living back in that area, too. There was a beautiful spring there near an apple tree. We went in this house, I'll never forget it. These mountain kids had white mice and they were everywhere."

Lacy said that another favorite ride on his pony was down the old trail road. This is the road that begins at the point where State Route 638 veers sharply to the left and heads into Blue Mountain. The old trail road goes on to Paris, Virginia.

"That is an interesting road and the old timers talked about deserters from the armies and escaped slaves going up in that area," he said.

One of the more surprising stories that Lacy heard was that deserters from the Revolutionary War, both the American side and the Tory side, escaped to the area of the trail road.

"This was a very wild area then with no trails. The story went that they deserted up here and lived off the land. They lived up in what is the Rock Spring area.

"There is an original old cabin there at Rock Spring that dates from Revolutionary War days. We used to go back and look at it when we were kids."

[My own research failed to turn up any definite data on Revolutionary War deserters on the trail road. However, there were deserters from both armies and a favorite place for any escapees, whether they be soldiers, slaves, or convicts, are wild isolated mountain areas. There were many instances of Hessian soldiers who were mercenaries for the British in the Revolutionary War, deserting the British army. Many Hessians were prisoners of the Americans in the Winchester area and many are known to have escaped and decided to stay, because they preferred the young America.]

"All of these mountain areas," Lacy said, "including this mountain were places where slaves escaped to before and during the Civil War," Lacy said.

"Over on Rattlesnake Mountain (a nearby mountain in Fauquier County) we have a community called 'Little Africa.' This is an area that was founded by escaped slaves. They were later joined by freed slaves. Some of the names up there are Jacksons, Washingtons, Baltimores, and Crisemon. These names go way back. There is an old Negro church up there. That community has practically disappeared, tho. A few families are still up there. Guy Jackson lives up there. And "Shoots" Crisemon, he's seventy-two now, he works for me here at Freezeland."

Farther up on Rattlesnake Mountain, U.S. Senator Russell Long of Louisiana had a summer home which commands a view of surrounding mountains.

Slaves worked and lived in the Blue Mountain area before the Civil War. The mountain was also a place where many slaves escaped to. The mountain used to have a much larger black population than it does today. On the road leading from Blue Mountain to Howellsville, for example, there used to be two black churches. One of these churches burned and the other, which is still standing was converted to a house.

Ben Lacy's childhood journey down the trail road led him to an actual landmark of the Civil War.

"Beyond the Rock Spring area, about another half-mile, you come to be a clearing called the Overlook. You get a very good view in both directions, to the west you see the Shenandoah Valley and to the east of the Piedmont area, toward Washington.

"Because of this excellent location this was used as a signal station, mostly by the South, in the Civil War. The main signal station was at Signal Knob on Massanutten Mountain. They would signal by mirrors from Massanutten to this mountain and, I am told, there would be signal stations at various high points all the way to Richmond."

There is a U.S. geodetic survey marker at the Overlook, today. The walk to the Civil War signal station, down the old trail road, is a favorite one for Blue Mountaineers and others. This road which was built by the C.C.C., was once part of the Appalachian Trail, but because of the increase in private owners, it is not used as much.

Lacy said that the Overlook is a favorite spot for Winchester artist John Chumley and other painters.

"As you know some of the best views of the Valley from the mountain are in the morning when the sun is behind it. The view becomes hazier as the day goes on and the sun goes down. From the overlook the artist can paint the clear views of the valley in the morning and, then, in the afternoon, he can turn eastward and paint the Piedmont, which in the morning is hazy, but it is clear in the afternoon."

An old CCC road that few people, even today, know exists was a favorite of Lacy on his pony rides. This road is off 638 about a 100 yards south of the towers, towards Linden. There is an entrance at the State Game Commission parking lot.

"This road led to Manor Leeds, at one time considered the largest apple orchard in the world," Lacy said.

In the summer of 1977 I walked down this road. It is a wondrous winding road through an unspoiled forests, filled on that day with colorful butterflies. At the end of the road my partner and myself came upon a clearing that afforded us one of the most marvelous views in our many years of tramping these Blue Ridge mountains. It overlooked the rolling hills, mountains, rich farmland and the blue grass of the Virginia countryside in Fauquier County. The view opened on to private property and, thanks to the graciousness of the owners, we were allowed to continue across their property on another road. This road took us to what appeared like a ghost town. There were several old, gray-wooded buildings. A little old vacant store that looked like it might have been a general store. There was a huge, ancient structure with four cupolas on top of it.

We were delighted to learn, later on, that we had stumbled on to the old buildings of the former, great Manor Leeds orchard. The large, ancient building was the old packing house where they sorted the apples. The apple trees, for the most part, are all gone. The orchard acreage had been replaced by the rolling rich farms and blue grass that we had seen in our magnificent view.

The choice of the name Manor Leeds for the orchard was an appropriate one. The orchard is on land that even today is called Leeds Manor. Leeds Manor was one of the large "Manors" designated in the time of Lord Fairfax, that was separated out of his huge five million acre land grant from the King of England. Leeds Manor was about 125,000 acres and part of its westerly line was Fauquier-Warren line which borders Blue Mountain. The Manor was in Fauquier County.

Another little used road that leads to an equally fascinating area is a road that begins just above where the Freezeland Orchard ends, on the way to Blue Mountain. It is the first State Game Commission parking lot on the right.

"Just as you get beyond the orchard on the right side, you'll see a road back in there. This is another road we used to ride down," Lacy said.

"This was called the oil factory road because it led to a small factory that made sassafras oil. They found a lot of sassafras trees back in there years ago. The extract gained from these trees eventually became the mixture for your soft drinks, your colas and root beers.

"If you walk down in there today you'll find a spring down in there and you find the ruins of the old chimney of the factory."

Lacy said, as far as he remembers, the oil factory was there about the turn of the century.

On the orchard property itself, Lacy said, is an old copper mine that dates back to Revolutionary War days.

"Geologists say that this land up on this mountain is all a copper stone, what they call a green stone. The ruins of the old mine are still there."

Lacy remembers when Henry de Longfief first purchased Blue Mountain.

"It was interesting because just prior to his purchase there had been a movement by the State of Virginia to purchase that whole area, what is now Blue Mountain, for a state park. What happened was that the state eventually purchased the land to the south and the east of Blue Mountain, that land that is in Fauquier County, for a state hunting preserve." Lacy said.

He remembered that the first vacation-home developer to come to this area was Jack Burrows, the developer of Skyland Estates.

"I believe it was about 1954 or 1955, when Burrows purchased land at the time the person who owned the land gave me a chance to buy it back. It was about 400 acres and the timber was all cut off of it. It had some beautiful views of the Valley. But it didn't lie to well for an orchard. And we had no need for pasture land. He sold it to Burrows for $6,000 and from that Burrows developed Skyland Estates.

"He was the first developer to come up here. It was actually his second development. His first one was Blue Ridge Estates."

Lacy remembers that when Burrows began Skyland he built an air strip up there and used to fly in frequently.

"I used it several times to have planes take off from there to spray the orchard," Lacy said.

At one point in my research and in talking to Lacy, I reflected on the many commercial enterprises that have taken place on the mountain. I was quite surprised to find that what appeared to be a quiet mountain area, turned out to have an amazing amount of activity in the past 250 years.

There is a good chance that the young George Washington or other colonial surveyors surveyed this mountain before the Revolutionary War. So, to begin with, it provided a source of income for colonial surveyors in the employ of Lord Fairfax.

Some of the other uses: copper mining, lumbering, oil factory (sassafras), apple and peach growing, barrel factory, beekeeping, whiskey making (both the legal and illegal kind) , and, up to this point, real estate and the building trades.

Ben Lacy has seen a lot of this. And his childhood memories, as he rode his pony down the old mountain trails, are where it all began.

- 13 -
LARRY LEHEW:
WELL-DRILLING, GEOLOGY, AND
AN ANTE-BELLUM Southern MANSION

Front Royal entreprenuer Larry Lehew is shown with one of his race horses at his stable at Bel Air. Lehew descends from the pioneer family of Front Royal and is a millionaire well-driller, horseman and musician.

Larry Lehew is a name that means many things in the Front Royal area. He is an eighth generation LeHew and his roots stretch way back to Peter LeHew, one of the founders of Front Royal.

He lives at Bel Air, a white-columned Southern mansion that Robert E. Lee visited after the battle of Gettysburg.

He rides his horse, along with Jackie Kennedy Onassis and others in the Rappahanock Hunt.

He is drilling wells at such a rapid rate these days, he has purchased another $400,000 rig just to keep up with the business. He now has three of these rigs. He has drilled more than 50 wells just at Blue Mountain. His vast experience in well-drilling makes him a valuable source of information to State of Virginia geologists. Most of the geological data about Blue Mountain, contained in this chapter, comes from LeHew and the state geologists.

And, on top of all this, the energetic LeHew is a prize-winning horseman, a band leader, a singer and an avid motorcyclist and a friend to the "famous" who have recently settle in the Shenandoah Valley, the Hunt Country and the Blue Ridge Mountains.

"I guess you could say I just love life. I like everything I'm doing-- my work, my family, people, horses, motorcycles, you name it," Lehew said.

Lehew, born in 1937, traces his ancestry back to a Front Royal tavernkeeper by the name of Peter Lehew. In fact, before the 1780's the community was known as Lehewtown, after Peter and his brother, Spencer, another innkeeper.

An insight into Larry Lehew's own likable, soaring spirits, may come with considering a closer relative, his grandfather, Frank Lehew.

"My grandfather, Frank Lehew, was probably the best Lehew known by name, but he never made any money and he didn't care if he didn't. He loved to have a good time," Lehew said.

"He was a hell of a dancer. That's all he was interested in. He would go to square dances whenever there was one. He was quite famous for that in this area.

"He sold Watkins products out of the trunk of his car. These were linaments and powders and he would travel down all of these country roads around here selling them to farmers. He was a farmer, himself most of his life."

WELL DRILLING

Lehew's knowledge of well-drilling comes from his father, Homer Lehew.

"My father was in the building business for many years in this area, starting back in the 1930's. He used to drill wells for the people he had built houses for. It took a lot longer in those days. While he was drilling a well he would board at the house where he was drilling. They could only get down about three to ten feet a day, then. With these new rigs we've got today we can go three hundred feet a day, even through solid rock. So you can see the difference.

"When my father was drilling he was using one of those old rope machines. I started on a cable machine and that is obsolete, now. My father used to drill ten to twelve wells a year. At my present rate, with my two rigs, I can drill two wells in one afternoon.

However, the new speed of drilling wells, also means a considerable outlay of money. Lehew recently paid $400,000 for his new rig.

The price of drilling wells varies, according to the county and the soil. Lehew charges $7 a foot in Faquier County, $7 a foot in Rappahanock County and $6.00 per foot at Blue Mountain. There is also an extra charge for encasing the well. At these rates, for example, a 300 foot well at Blue Mountain would cost between $2,500 and $3,000. (These are 1991 prices).

[Note - These prices will change- Waiting for call from Larry]

He has been drilling wells on the mountain called Blue Mountain before it had that name. One of his toughest jobs, he remembers, was drilling the well for the American Telephone and Telegraph tower on top of the mountain in 1956.

"We spent the whole winter up on the mountain on that one. That is another example of how things have changed in the past twenty years. Like most of Blue Mountain it was rocky in that area. With the equipment we had then, a cable rig, we could only go three feet in a 10-hour day.

"When we'd get offers to do some of those mountain jobs we'd usually say we were too busy to do them. But, really, we just didn't like all of that rock. Well, on that job we finally struck water at one hundred and fifty feet. But it took us all winter. Today, we can drill a three-hundred foot well in a rocky, mountain area in one day."

Lehew drilled the well at Henry and Colette de Longfief's home. That was more than thirty years ago and that well is still coming in fine." That well was 130 feet.

Lehew grew up in the Front Royal area and went to high school there. When he was growing up his father was in the construction business. He used to accompany his father on construction and well-drilling jobs. So he got a general knowledge of how things operated. However, shortly after he graduated from high school in 1955, his father left the construction business and built a motel, Cool Harbor, in Front Royal.

"I realized then that I really didn't have any way of making a living. I think I was planning on going in the contruction business with my father. And now that was gone.

"But along about that time an interesting thing happened. Harold Marency, he's the fellow that built President Kennedy's house near Middleburg, called me. Marency had his own home in Marshall. He said he wanted a well drilled. I had a little experience in this working during the summertime. But I'd never actually done the whole thing myself.

"Well, daddy's old well machine was sitting there in the yard. I took it down to Marency's place and started to work with it. I drilled him a well, with that old machine. We went down about a hundred feet. I think we got about ten gallons in a minute.

"I'll never forget the next part. Marency came out of the door. And I showed him the water coming up. He said: "Well, who should I make the check out to?"

"I had to think for a minute. Then I said, 'Well, I did the work Just make it out to me.' They've been making them out to me ever since."

Lehew remembers that he charged six dollars a foot for that first well.

But the gregarious, outgoing Larry Lehew didn't limit himself to drilling wells.

"I had always been interested in music, since I was a kid. I played trumpet and the drums. I remember playing in a band in a night club when I was fourteen or fifteen. I used to have friends the same age playing, too. Our mothers and fathers used to come down and listen to us. They would sit outside and listen to us.

"Then as the years went by, when I got in to my twenties, I formed my own band. I used to lead the band and sing. We played all over this area -- Front Royal, Winchester, Frederick. It was the rock and roll era. But you could say we played whatever was on the top forty whether it was rock, country, or soft music."

The name of the band was "Larry and the Shadows." He had the band from 1960 to 1972.

"In 1969 I started to get interested in raising horses and fox hunting. So about that time I was drilling wells, running the band and fox hunting. Something had to give. I couldn't stay up all nights, singing in the band and get up the next morning and drill wells or hunt foxes."

But he loves to sing and when he is at a party in the Front Royal-Winchester area he is always asked to sing. He had a lot of nostalgia for the old band days. He still kept it up for a number of years. "Once a few years back we got the old band together and we played a dance together with the 'Platters.' We hadn't been together in six or seven years. They'd printed 500 tickets, but 650 showed up."

Larry recently resurrected the band and called it: "The Silver Shadows." Omega Records of Kensington, Md. came out with a new album for the band that contains ten new selections. The band has had engagements in the Shenandoah Valley, Maryland, Washington D.C., Virginia and the West Virginia areas.

He was formerly married to Nancy Jane Richardson. They have a son Jefferey, who is the owner of VIA Satellites in Front Royal and a daughter Wendy, a flight attendant with US Air.

In 1977 Larry and Jeff won a joint prize at the prestigious Rappahanock Hunt Point-to-Point races. Their trophy was presented to them by U.S. Senator and former Secretary of the Navy John Warner and his then wife, Elizabeth Taylor.

LeHew's well-drilling and fox hunting brings him into contact with the celebrity world of the Hunt Country. He makes friends easily in this world and numbers among his friends, besides the Warners, Ray Scherrer, Bill Monroe and the late Frank McGee of NBC TV. Scherrer and Monroe, former NBC-TV brodcasters, and David Brinkley, also of NBC-TV, Washington, all have homes in nearby Rappahanock County. LeHew drilled wells for Scherrer, Monroe and McGee.

Larry has been friends with Jackie Kennedy Onassis for several years. Mrs. Onassis has been coming to the Virginia Hunt Country for many years. She and her late husband, President John F. Kennedy, built a home near Atoka in the early 1960s. LeHew sees Mrs. Onassis at several of the Rappahanock and Orange County hunts. He is also a friend of former Senator Eugene McCarthy, who has a home in Rappahanock. One of his prize posessions is an autographed copy of a Senator McCarthy book of poems.

The affluent society of Washington, D.C. area is having a powerful effect on the beautiful mountainous Virginia counties where the LeHews grew up.

The wealthy, the famous and the middle income Washington-area person, more and more, are choosing to build second homes in Fauquier, Warren, Loudon and Rappahanock Counties and other nearby areas. Warren County, for example, (where Front Royal is the county seat) is expected to nearly double it's population in the next 20 years, making it one of the fastest growing counties in Virginia. Most of this growth will be people moving out from the Washington area, either to commute to work or to retire.

"When they gave the go ahead on route 66 I knew that was time for me to buy a new drilling rig," LeHew said.

In 1991 Lehew will drill about 250 wells. But with the new rig and the new help he plans to employ he could drill 400 wells a year.

Does he always strike water when he drills?

"No, not all of the time. But I guess you could say most of the time. But that's what makes well-drilling so interesting, you never know what is going to happen."

Lehew said that a lot of people will not drill for water until they first have a "water witch" test for water.

What is a water witch?

"Well," Lehew said, "I call them water witch, but the correct name is dowsers. They go around your property

with a green forked stick or nylon rod. They think they can find water.

"I don't believe in all of that stuff. But a lot of people swear by them, a lot of educated people, too. They won't drill a well before the water witch comes.

"A peach limb is a favorite stick. In fact," Lehew said, with a smile, "a water witch comes by my place and gets willow branches down here along the creek.

"Scientifically, water doesn't attract. So I don't know what happens. I can get it to work for me, too. But, I don't like to. Say the stick says it's here and then I drill 500 feet and no water comes up. Then that gets me in hot water."

Does any piece of land look better to him than another, when he is looking for water?

"It is always nice when I go in a place to see springs and hand dug wells around. That means there should be water there. It is a good sign."

LeHew said that the Blue Mountain area fooled him several times.

"I used to think that if we didn't hit water up there at 250 to 300 feet that we wouldn't get any and we might as well try another place. But the last few years have disproved that. In recent years we have gone from 400 to 450 feet on Blue Mountain and hit ten to fifteen gallons a minute. That is very good for a house.

"Usually the deeper you go the less chance you have of hitting water. You don't hit as many cracks and the water is running in those cracks.

"Most of the time you'll get a sign. If your rock is changing colors it is a good sign. If it is going from green to blue, blue to red, then you want to continue drilling.

"When you start to get white quartzite rock, every now and then, a real white rock, that's a good sign you'll generally get water. I don't care how deep you are," LeHew said.

On the other hand, Lehew said, if the rock is identical, if there is no change in color, no cracks in the rock structure, there is little likelihood that water will be found.

However, LeHew said, even this theory is open to question.

"We had a good example of that on Blue Mountain just recently. We were down 225 feet. We weren't getting any water at all. The same rock structure, no change. So the young man drilling the well said:

"Where do you want to drill the next hole? We aren't going to get any water in this well."

"I said to continue because we had hit water nearby at 400 feet and you just never know. They went to 245 feet and they broke the bit off the drill. (The sharp, front part of the drill.) Well, they had to go back to Front Royal to get a tool to get that bit out. Ordinarily they wouldn't try to get that bit out if we didn't think we were going to get water. Well, at 345 feet we hit water at twenty gallons a minute:

"That goes to show you that you just never know. That is what is so interesting about drilling. you can do it day in and day out -- By golly you just don't know."

Lehew said that there are three wells close together at Blue Mountain. One struck water at 180 feet, another at 345 feet and another at 400 feet.

"And these wells are just fifty feet apart. You just never know," he said.

How do you explain water? Are there rivers underneath the earth?

"Yes," LeHew said, "you could put it that way. But where they are, at what depth, is a mystery.

"But one thing is certain. Your drill has got to hit a crack in the rock where the water is flowing through. Now that crack could be at one hundred feet or at five hundred feet. But if you don't hit that crack you won't find water."

At a point in the drilling process, he said, "you hit bed rock."

This is a point when you start to drill through a layer of solid rock.

"This is another mystery, tho. Sometimes you hit bed rock at twenty feet. At other times, in the same general area on Blue Mountain it may be down a hundred feet."

Where bed rock is located is important to a well driller because that determines how much casing is to be used in the well.

"To start with," Lehew said, "we drill a ten inch, in diameter hole. In the beginning we are drilling through dirt, loose rock and there may be some surface water. Now this surface water may contain some bacteria. So, as we say we have to 'case' this out. But we are not sure that we will be free of surface water, loose dirt and rock until we hit bed rock. The pipe that your water flows through is 6-5/8 inches in diameter. This pipe will have a protective casing around as far down as the bedrock surface. But, as I say, we don't know when we'll hit bed rock, sometimes at twenty feet, sometimes as deep as one hundred feet," he said.

Lehew said there is an old myth about bed rock:

"You hear the old timers say when you get through that bed rock that you hit water. Well, I would like to know when that is because it never happens. It is solid bedrock from here to the other end of the earth."

Health laws in regard to wells are stricter in some counties than they are in others. Some counties close to Warren County have a grout law. This means that after the casing is in, down to the bed rock, cement has to be poured into the space between the 10 inch hole and the 6-5/8 casing. This gives greater assurance that surface water will not seep into the well. Warren County, as yet, does not have a grout law.

GEOLOGY

Well drillers provide invaluable information for the State of Virginia geologists.

"They are interested in wells in different areas. So I might spend a day with them and we will ride around to Fort Valley, Flint Hill and Blue Mountain. I will tell them how far down I went, at what point I hit bedrock, how much water, how many gallons per minute came up, the type of rock we went through," LeHew said. He said that all well drillers are now required to keep a log on each well they drill and include the foregoing information.

A recent State of Virginia publication entitled, "Geology of the Linden and Flint Hill Quadrangles" (1976) states that the bed rock in the Blue Mountain area (Linden Quadrangle) ranges in age from the Precambrian to Mesozoic period.

This makes the rock structure at Blue Mountain part of the earliest geological era or some of the "oldest rocks in the world."

The rocks in the Blue Mountain Area are of the Cattootin Formation. They are described as "massive, dark to grayish-green metabasalt."

The Blue Ridge Mountains form the major drainage divide in the State of Virginia. Water from the creeks and springs on Blue Mountain flows northwest to the Shenandoah River. The Shenandoah flows northeasterly to Harper's Ferry where it meets the Potomac on its journey to Chesapeake Bay and eventually to the Atlantic Ocean. The streams draining southeast of the mountain flow into the Rappahanook River which also makes its way to the bay and then the ocean.

There was a time, millions of years ago, when the Blue Ridge mountains were underneath a vast inland ocean. It is fascinating to see recently dug up fossils, with the imprint of clam shells from that era.

Maurice Brooks, in his book "The Appalachians" (Seneca Books) gives an interesting description of the "old" mountains.

"The true Appalachians begin tentatively, with broken and isolated masses of ancient metamorphic rock, followed by low but continuous ridged, such as Maryland's Catoctins.

"Then, with little that is premonitory, soared the Blue Ridge, a real mountain chain which breaks horizons from Pennsylvania to Georgia. In the southern portion of the Appalachian system, the Blue Ridge is the heart of 'Old' Appalachia. All its rocks are enduring, resistant to erosion, and therefore bald and steep."

In recent years there have been some startling archeological discoveries in the Front Royal area. Down along the Shenandoah River, in areas where Larry Lehew and other Front Royalers played as children, an 11,000 year old Indian village has been unearthed at Flint Run.

Dr. William Gardner, Chairman of the Anthropology Department at Catholic University, who is in charge of the Flint Run digs, said the discovery is significant because the settlement was so large and that much of its valuable artifacts have remained undisturbed for so many years.

"No place like this can be found in North America. This site is unique because we can get at their total way of life," Gardner told Washington Post Reporter Bart Barnes in an interview in May of 1971.

The site where the village was found is seven miles south of Front Royal, near Limeton, Virginia, along the banks of the river near an old rock quarry.

The first clues that there was something important came in 1969 when members of the Shenandoah Valley Chapter of the Virginia Archeological Association discovered stone arrow and spear tips in the cornfield near the quarry. The artifacts were displayed at the annual exhibit of the association in Winchester. They eventually came to the attention of Garner, who launched the expedition. Each summer students from Catholio University carefully sift the dirt at the site. These Paleo-Indian artifacts, stone tools, are the oldest found in North America, Garner said.

BEL AIR, THE ANTE-BELLUM SOUTH

Of all the fascinating things that Larry Lehew has done in his life, by far the most interesting was his purchase of Bel Air, the historic old Southern mansion of Front Royal.

The visitor to Bel Air today can stand between its magnificent white pillars and gaze off in the distance at the mountains all around and imagine the excitement and terror that the Civil War brought to the little town down below. For Bel Air had an authentic "Old South" family that gave its all to the Confederacy: a fiery, Southern belle Lucy Buck was its most expressive resident, writing a diary as the Civil War cannons boomed around her; and the most revered man of the south, General Robert E. Lee visited from Gettysburg.

The purchase of Bel Air by the Lehews was a journey back into history for the Lehew family. The land that Bel Air is located on was originally owned by Peter Lehew more than 200 years ago.

"It is one of the most vivid books I have ever read on the Civil War. It gives you a very personal perspective, of how the war affected a small Southern town and the lives of a Southern family," Larry Lehews said.

Bel Air is located on an elevation above Front Royal off the Happy Creek road. Lucy, writing in her diary in the winter of 1861, tells about her view from the front of the house and about the "blue mountains."

"The evening was lovely and I turned to look on the landscape spread before me. In the foreground the smooth lawn-like meadows and the little Happy Creek like a silver thread meandering through them.

"Then the quiet village with the crimson sunset on its windows, and its bright wreaths of curling smoke, and beyond the undulating hill -- and in the distance like a fitting frame to this sweet picture stretched the blue mountains all with a cloudless heaven overhead painted with the sunset pencils...."

The "quiet village" consisted of about "five hundred inhabitants, including slaves" in 1861. Many of the Buck relatives lived in similar great houses in Front Royal and the surrounding area.

The late Laura Viginia Hale of Front Royal, the diligent historian of the Civil War in the Northern Shenandoah Valley (author of "Four Valiant Years") said that "although Yankees by the thousands" marched through and fought over the Valley they never "conquered the irrepressible Lucy."

Lucy, Miss Hale writes, in a preface to the book, whether "gleeful or gloomy she is ever valuable whether describing a very exciting, very exhilarating battle with bullets and shells passing near enough to whisper confidential messages or whether enjoying merry gatherings (at Bel Air) around tea table, piano or fireside with soldiers camped nearby or home on leave, hungry for food, flirtation or family."

Miss Hale also writes:

"As a rail and crossroads town, Front Royal was often a hive of military operations and excitement, lying in the path of armies advancing with bands playing and flags flying, and in the wake of the wounded and weary backwash of such tragic encounters as Antietam and Gettysburg.

"Bel Air, as the mansion house of a productive farm of several hundred acres, a mill, and orchard in the 1860's, was occupied as headquarters for military staffs and campground for armies, Blue and Gray.

"Lucy's diary resounds with the marching feet and rolling wheels of 'might multitudes' filing past Bel Air."

As the terrible war continued Lucy's diary became more somber as the weary Southern soldiers came back from the front, wounded and hungry. Many of them were housed, fed and had their wounds treated at Bel Air. The old house, like many others in the Valley, was periodically converted to a hospital to care for the injured.

July 22, 1863 is an important date in Lucy's diary. General Robert E. Lee, on his return to Virginia, from the fateful battle.

Lucy writes that General Lee asked for "a Rebel song" and she and her sister Nellie played the piano and sang for them.

"I know," she writes, "General L. wished to know if we were not afraid to let those treasonable songs resound beneath our roof such as the "War Chant of Defiance."

Before leaving, General Lee signed Lucy and Nellie's autograph book.

Laura Hale, in writing of Lucy Buck:

"Charming, vivacious and popular, she had many beaux but never married. Continuing her diary she was a long-remembered and beloved figure as she sat with pad on her knee, in the midst of a chattering group of young relatives or in the quiet of her room."

Lucy Buck died in 1918. She is buried in Prospect Hill Cemetery Front Royal, a cemetery that holds many Civil War dead.

It was the dream of the Lehews to own the beautiful Bel Air, the site of so much Front Royal history, happiness and sadness. The purchase was made in 1973 from the Downing family. The Lehews then set in motion a major refurbishing, to restore the old mansion to its former glory. They also added some rooms. They spent several thousand dollars on this project. Stables were added and a recreation room, where parties and dances are held, was added above the barn. They moved to Bel Air in 1975.

Bel Air is the one house not to be missed on the annual Warren County house tour. After visitors see the beautiful old home and take advantage of the panoramic view from its veranda they can go up into the Bel Air attic. There, on the ceiling, they will find the pre-Civil War markings of Lucy Rebecca Buck.

- 13 - A -
Lehew Family History

(This chapter was written in 1991)

Speech given by Larry Lehew on the occasion of the Festival Of Leaves October, 1990. Eighth generation descendent of Peter LeHew, founder of LeHewtown, now Front Royal.

I was asked to come here this morning to tell about the founding of our town Front Royal. I'll have to say as you are about to find out that I'm not very good at this sort of thing, but I'm kind of like the fellow that the judge gave 99 years. The fellow said, "Well your honor, I'm already 85 years old and I don't think I'm going to be able to do the time." So the judge said, "Just do the best you can."

Nicholas Lehew was from France, he was a Huguenot. He came first to England and then to the colony of Virginia. The exact date is not known, but there are records in the court house in Williamsburg that prove he was here in the 1680's. He had a son named Peter. The records show that Peter Lehew was appointee or agent of Virginia. He was clerk of the Privy Council or Solicitor of records in the colony. On file in Williamsburg are numerous entries made by him. One of his duties was levying and collecting taxes on liquor. He also attended to the disbursement of the funds, for example, it was up to him to decide how much money the College of William and Mary would receive. He was also responsible for obtaining and purchasing the portraits of the King and Queen to hang in the Capitol of the Colony.

George Washington did not survey all the land around here, Peter Lehew was a surveyor, maybe even more significant than Washington. At a council meeting held at the Capitol in 1727 the Governor laid before the board a letter from Peter Lehew, Solicitor of Viriginia affairs, dated the 24th of June 1727 on account of sundry fees and other charges expended by him in establishing the border between North Carolina and Virginia. There are numerous letters on record from his Majesty, The King of England, praising Peter Lehew for the speedy settlement of the boundaries of numerous counties in Virginia.

In 1733 the Privy Council of which Peter Lehew was a member issued an order directing the government to approve a commission to ascertain the real boundaries of the Fairfax properties, which includes 5,300,000 acres of the Northern Neck. This land was bounded by the Chesapeake Bay, the Potomac River, the Rapidan, the Rappahannock within the boundaries of our present counties of Northumberland, Lancaster, Westmoreland, Richmond, Stafford, King George,

Prince William, Fairfax, Loudoun, Fauquier, Rappahannock, Culpeper, Madison, Clarke, Warren, Page, Shenandoah and Frederick in Virginia. Hardy, Hampshire, Morgan, Beckeley and Jefferson in West Virginia.

An entry made in 1783 states that Lord Fairfax appeared before the Committee for Trade and Peter LeHew appeared on behalf of the Colony. I don't know whether these two struck some kind of deal under the table or what, but Lehew ended up with 972 acres granted to him from Lord Fairfax. All of this is on record in Prince William County because that is where the 972 acres was located. He sold this land in 1736 to a man named Alexander Scott. I guess he took his money that he got from Scott for his 972 acres and he bought 200 acres right where we are standing from a man named Christopher Marr. Marr had bought 400 acres from a man named William Russell. Russell got it from Lord Fairfax. Evidently these three men knew each other. Lehew bought the land from Marr in 1754, this is on record. By this time Lehew had several married children. We know that Lehew was hanging out around here in 1748, but it was not until 1754 that he established a permanent residence here, bringing his married children and their families here establishing LeHewtown.

All these years he co ntinued as an agent of the King in Virginia and he maintained his title of Clerk of the English Privy Council, but in March 1759 after 37 years of devotion and loyal service to the Crown he resigned. Now, I would think the reason for that would be the commute. His headquarters was still in Williamsburg and he was here. That would be a lot of windshield time even today, could you imagine what it would have been like back then?

In 1760 he obtained a license to operate an Ordinary, I guess that's the same thing as a fast house or a beer joint today. By then Lehewtown was growing. I guess just like people are attracted here now, they were then also.

Peter Lehew's will was recorded in Frederick County in 1780 and was signed by him. His wife, Frances and son David were named as his Executors. Nine of his eleven children were named as heirs. Some of them evidently thought their land was too small, so they moved away. Today if you go to big cities like Dallas or Los Angeles you may find one Lehew. There is only one Lehew for every quarted of a million Americans. There are not very many. Thank God for that, huh?

In 1788 the town was incorporated and the name was changed from LeHewtown to Front Royal. There are several stories about how we got the name Front Royal. Some of you know the one about fronting the Royal Oak. That was about Thomas Buck, when he was trying to drill a group of men to fight in the revolution. They wouldn't get the instructions straight, so Mr. Buck got frustrated and told them to turn around and Front the Royal Oak.

Now the things that I've told you this morning are on record in various court houses, but the story about the name change is not. We don't know if it is true or not.

If I may speculate on my own maybe it got it's name because it was a Frontier town. Front Royal has always been a little different from neighboring towns. I think we've always had the feeling of Independence, maybe even of dissent.

The Lehews didn't want to go along with the religious persecutions in France, so they came to England and then to here. Maybe the people here during those times were divided on the revolution, maybe they were divided on religion, maybe being situated where we are they may have been divided on the Civil War. They were independent, maybe even the Lehew family could have been divided. After all, Peter Lehew was a clerk of the king. He has a good job working for the King of England and yet at least two of his sons fought in the Revolution against England. The feeling of Independence, I think has always been evident here in Front Royal, and still is.

Maybe the Royal part of the name was the beginning of the end for Royal influence on us. Therefore, Front Royal, I think, is still a Frontier town. Not settled like some other Virginia towns, still changing, still growing, and taking Independence. There is an old saying, it's what's up front that counts. So Front Royal, I think reflects the spirit of the Lehew family over 200 years ago and I think it reflects the spirit of the native people living here now. Whenever you go somewhere people always want to know where you are from. When you say you are from Front Royal, Virginia they always seem to take special notice. Unless I get run out of town I think I'll always live here. There has been a Lehew here for well over 200 years. I hope 200 years from now there is still one here. Hopefully, it will be me!

*Marion and Al White, both formerly identified with the Linden Post-Office,
are long-time residents and experts on the history of the mountain area.*

- 14 -
THE WHITES: LINDEN, WHEN IT WAS A BUSTLING TOWN

Linden, Virginia, today, appears to be a sleepy, tree-shaded village in rural Virginia.

Of course, there is some bustle out where route 55 meets route 638, the road to Blue Mountain and Skyland Estates. People make last minute stops at Heflin's Grovery store before they drive up to their mountain homes.

But most people never see the real Linden which is on the other side of the road, south of 55, tucked away, like something out of a pleasant 19th Century past.

"You can't realize how busy Linden was in the Nineteen Twenties. It was really a small commercial center because of the Southern Railroad. It is hard to believe that today." The speaker is Alfred White, 75, of Linden. He should know. The Whites trace their ancestry back in Warren County for many years before that. Al's wife, Marion, the former Linden postmistress, also has deep roots.

But why was Linden such a busy center seventy years ago? "You've got to remember," Al said "in the Twenties what is now Blue Mountain was being lumbered by James McDonald and his sons. It was a common sight to see logs being hauled out of the mountains by horses to Linden.

"Freezeland Orchard was shipping apples all over the world. (First to England and later Argentina) Piedmont was also a big orchard. And my father had an orchard, too. "And, of course, years before that a dairy operated on the property we now own, separating the milk from the cream and sending the cream to Washington.

"This was a cattle area and their was a slaughterhouse nearby, east of here, on route 55. Farmers would drive their cattle up here from Rappahannock County. The slaughterhouse would later become a distillery.

"All of these enterprises used the railroad: lumber people, orchards, cattle, dairy, slaughterhouse. All of these products went by rail.

"Why I remember when I was growing up in the Twenties there were five sotres in Linden and two blacksmiths," Al said. "Everybody used the railroad then," Marion chimed in. "The teachers for the Linden school would come in on the morning train from Front Royal and leave on the afternoon train." I told them I heard there was a distillery over at Howellsville, too.

"Well, not legally," Al said, smiling.

"They were making it (moonshine) all over these hills," Marion laughed

"That's how these mountain people survived – making moonshine."

There was a summer boarder business, too. People would come out from Washington on the railroad to breathe the cooler mountain air. They would stay for weeks at a time. The Heflin family, Al said, built a house especially for summer boarders.

Wapping, one of the ante-bellum Warren County homes, near Linden, was used for summer boarders at one time.

Wapping can be seen from route 55 or from the newly-paved Dismal Hollow Road. It is a short distance west of Linden. It is one of the most historic homes in Warren County and was used as a hospital during the Civil War.

Historian Laura Virginia Hale in her book: "Four Valiant Years" wrote that "Wapping, home of John Hansbrough was used as a temporary hospital for the wounded and 'tis said so many amputated limbs were thrown into the icehouse that Mrs. Hansbrough could never get the consent of her mind to use it again."

Al and Marion White live in Linden in a beautiful 125-year old house high atop a hill generally in the area just north of 55.

Al's father, Charles White, was born in the family home, Shannon, near the Shenandoah River in 1880. His mother Lavinia Warner Dudley White was born in 1887 in Rappahannock County.

The Whites moved to Linden in 1915 and Al was born in their home in Linden in 1916.

The land that Al's father, Charles White, purchased in 1915 was part of a huge tract of land that at one time was owned by Richard Dulany. As we meantioned in an earlier chapter on Freezeland Orchard, the Crawford brothers and William C. White (no relation to Charles White) purchased the Freezeland property in 1906, from Dulany.

In 1915, Al said, his father purchased about 600 acres which later became their home property. The purchase, according to Al White was made from a man by the name of Mobes, who had been a Washington developer. Mobes had purchased it from another landowner who had bought it from Richard Dulany.

A vivid reminder of the Dulany days, which date to before the Civil War, is the old stone dairy that still stands and has been converted into a cozy one bedroom home by Al and Marion White. Their son, Alfred Lewis White, Jr., a Front Royal lawyer and his wife, Jean, occupied the "dairy house" for several months before they built their own home in Front Royal. An icehouse and a barn where the dairy cows were kept also still stand.

The beautiful old home where the Whites have lived most of their married life was originally the tenant house on the dairy farm. It is estimated that the house is more than 125 years old which would put its construction about the time of the Civil War.

Thw Whites were married in 1947.

"I didn't want to live in the tenant house. There just wasn't much to it at the time. It was only a small place and no one had lived in it for years. I wanted to fix up the dairy. But Al insisted and so we decided on this house." Marion said. They turned the small tenant house into a substantial beautiful home surrounded by evergreen trees.

"That tree," Marion said pointing to a giant evergreen in front of the house, "is 35 years old. I remember when we planted it."

Al White has fond memories of growing up in a Linden that was radically different than it is today.

"In the Twenties there were four passenger trains a day through Linden and the train depot was the center of activity. As I said there were a lot of products going out of here by rail –lumber, fruit, dairy products, cattle. In its own way it was a busy place. But there weren't so many cars and a lot of people rode horses or ponies. My brother rode his horse to school in Front Royal every day.

"But the old railroad station was torn down years ago," Al said.

If you liked to hunt or trap Linden was a great place to be in the old days.

"Trapping was a source of income," Al recalled. "We set traps for skunks, muskrat, fox, possum, and occasionally we would get a mink."

How much would you get for a mink?

"Mink were the most expensive. They'd go anywheres from eighteen to thirty dollars. But in those days, in the depression, that was a lot of money."

Al said that he saw a fox recently but he hasn't seen a mink in several years.

Marion said the reason there were very few wild animals around was:

"For one thing we are not attractive for wild animals anymore because it used to be that everyone had chickens and guineas and ducks and they had a few sheep and a few cows. These are the type of animals that a fox would prey upon and now no one has farm animals anymore. We used to keep a couple of cows. Now you never hear a cow 'moo' anymore.

"Ralph Morris, up on Freezeland, has a few cows. But that's about all around here. This used to be great sheep country. When I was child, every night, at one time, a chicken would disappear. Then we set a trap just outside of the chicken pen and we caught one of these big 'hoo hoo' owls—a horned owl- he was coming in and carrying a chicken off every night," she related.

When the White property was purchased in 1914 the Whites and Lee Sowers, a farmer, joined in the purchase, Al related. "Mr. Sowers took the top half of the property, because he had a flock of sheep he wanted to graze. My father took the bottom half of the property which had the old dairy farm on it. It also had a new house on it that had been built by Mr. Mobes. This is the house I was born in and my mother lived there until recently," Al said.

One of Al's early childhood memories was an all-day experience involving Mr. Sowers' sheep.

"Where Mister Sowers grazed his sheep later became Skyland Estates. In the Twenties he would call over here and ask father if us boys could help him round up those sheep. Mister Sowers had twelve or thirteen children and they would help out, too. We would all go up and round up those sheep and drive 'em on down to the cattle pens in Linden. There they picked out the best lambs they wanted to sell. We brought the sheep to the pens around this old barn that had a dipping vat and we put all these sheep through this sheep dip. After we got them all dipped we'd take them back up on the mountain. That was quite a day's work," Al said.

While Al was growing up in Linden Marion was going to school in Browntown.

"When I was growing up Front Royal was a small town of about two thousand people," Marion said.

"I can remember when people rode horses to town, it was that rural," she said.

Marion's family moved to Linden after she graduated from high school and that is when she got to know Al. When World War II broke out Al went into the Field Artilley and served in New Guinea.

After the war, in 1947, Marion and Al were married. They have three children: the previously mentioned Alfred "Chip" White and two daughters. Deborah W. Orsi and Mary Lavinia White. Both of the Whites have had long identification with the U.S. Postal Service in Linden. Al was a carrier since 1950 and Marion was a cleark in the postoffice and then, in 1970, Marion was appointed postmistress. She held that position until her retirement in 1980. The Whites' long history in the area and their positions with the postoffice in Linden gave them a unique knowledge of the community.

They remember when the de Longfiefs first came to this area in 1955.

"Why there wasn't anyone on that mountain when the de Longfiefs came here, except the McDonalds hauling their lumber and Charlie Reynolds way over on the other side," Al said. Although Blue Mountain was considered a quiet development, a community devoted to peaceful mountain living, it was also the precursor of great changes in the Linden area. Many more, not so quiet developments, were to follow.

The biggest development was super highway route 66, which literally cut the White's property in half.

"We're on this side of 66 and my parents home is on the other side," Al said. Thirty five acres, right in the center of the White property were taken to the contruct 66 through Linden. Although the White property is relatively peaceful, still, you can hear the sounds of traffic, especially tractor-trailers off in the distance, traversing 66.

Blue Mountain and Skyland Estates, when they were being developed in the 50s. Attracted retirees from the Washington area and people who liked to have weekend and vacation homes on the mountain. The population explosion in Warren County, caused mainly by 66, has brought a much younger age group to the mountain. With the average home price in the Washington, D.C. area at $500,000 and up many young couples despair of ever owning a home. With the prices of many Blue Mountain and Skyland Estates homes in the $50,000 to $75,000 bracket they became quite attractive to young couples just starting out. Marion has many fond memories of her days at the Postoffice. "The Appalachian Trail, from Maine to Georgia, isn't too far away from the Postoffice. I certainly met a lot of interesting people of all ages who would stop off in Linden to get supplies.

One hiker, during the school year, looked young enough to be in school.

"I said to him: 'Shouldn't you be in school?'

"He said: 'I took a year off. I want to find myself.'

"I thought that was kind of funny, trying to find himself on the trail."

The Whites view all of this progress with mixed emotions. It is like the difference between the chain saw and the axe.

"Years ago," Al said, as he looked over the mountains on a brisk fall day, you would hear the sound of the axe. Someone chopping firewood for the winter nights. Now all you hear is the greedy sound of chain saws. Somehow, I liked the sound of the axe. It was more peaceful."

Trappist Brother James Sommers of Holy Cross Abbey, near Berryville, has unearthed Indian artifacts that are estimated to be 10,000 years old. He has also found enough battle shells and bullets on the monastery grounds to establish the location there of a Civil War battle.

- 15 -
SOLDIERS, MONKS
AND THE SHENANDOAH

A short trip from Blue Mountain is a monastery that can trace its roots back to St. Benedict in Sixth Century Europe.

Visitors to my house on Blue Mountain would receive a special Sunday morning treat. We would drive over to Berryville to hear the old Latin Mass sung, in Gregorian chant, by the Trappist monks of Holy Cross Abbey.

The monks still sing the Mass. But now it is in English. Over the years I had learned a lot about the Trappists at the Abbey and their long, rich tradition. But it was only recently that I heard about the Abbey's connection to the Civil War.

The late Pat Murray, a Washington friend, made regular retreats at the monastery. On one visit she noticed a confederate flag near the desk of one of her Trappist friends. Knowing that the priest was from the North she was curious about a Yankee having a Confederate flag.

"Didn't you know, Pat," he said, "that a Civil War battle was fought on the monastery grounds? Every July 18, the date of the battle, we raise the Confederate flag and the American flag, in memory of the men who died here in 1864."

Pat passed on this information to me. That led me to spend a pleasant and informative morning with Brother James Sommers, the resident Trappist expert on not only that Civil War battle but he is also an enthusiastic anthropologist who has discovered hundreds of Indian artifacts along the shore of the west bank of the Shenandoah River. The river forms the eastern boundary of the 1200 acre abbey which is about 65 miles west of Washington, off route 7.

We were standing in the old Mansion House, an 18th Century home, and Brother James has a large, green, stone object in his hand.

"This is an Indian flake axe," he said.

"It is one of the oldest axes I have. It dates to the early archaic period which would be between eight and six thousand years, B.C.

"It is one of the oldest stone tools. It could be ten thousand years old."

Brother James is an example of a curious person, who through patience and persistence has made some interesting discoveries.

Trappist monks spend their days in prayer and work. For most of their time in the monastery they observe the rule of silence, except, as in Brother James case, when they are relating to the public. Holy Cross Abbey, near Berryville, was founded in 1950. Brother James was assigned here, from another monastery, in 1968.

"I used to take long walks near the river and from time to time, during these walks I would come up with some curious objects. I had a feeling that this area was once an Indian hunting or an Indian campground.

"After I had picked up several of these objects I decided to do something about it. I decided to find someone who could help me identify some of these articles."

Fortunately for Brother James, Dr. William Gardner, chairman of the Department of Anthropology at Catholic University in Washington, had taken an intense interest in the early life along the Shenandoah River. South of Front Royal, along the river, evidence of an actual Indian village has been found. Dr.Gardner began Thunderbird Museum on the site of the village. The discoveries at Thunderbird are dealt with in Chapter 13.

Dr. Gardner came out to the Abbey and was delighted to see the progress made by Brother James. Because of the great amount of artifacts found by Brother James the monastery grounds have been registered as an official anthropological site.

Was there an actual village here, I asked, like Thunderbird?

"No, we don't think it was a village. But it certainly was a campground and hunting area. These Indians were hunter-gatherers. They moved around a lot. The reason I found so much is they were traveling back and forth," he said.

Brother James said the flake axe would have been a tool used to clear land. The second tool he displayed was a notch axe which would have been about six thousand years old. A four thousand year old axe which he displayed would have been used to take the hide off an animal and other scraping uses.

Brother James has a large collection of projectile points, commonly known as arrowheads.

He also said that New York State Indians visited here because he found artifacts identified as being from those areas. I was especially interested in this because my hometown, Syracuse, N.Y. was the headquarters of the Onondaga Indians, the central tribe of the great Iroquois Federation.

One of Brother James' projectile points was labeled "Brewerton," which is a community near Syracuse on Oneida Lake, the general area of the Oneida Indians, another tribe of the Iroquois Federation.

The Trappists have been here, as was mentioned, since 1950. But the house—the Mansion House—where the anthropological and Civil War displays are located, dates to 1784. The house was built by John Wormley.

"Ralph Wormley, John's father, got this land at an auction at Williamsburg, Virginia in Seventeen Forty," Brother James said.

He paid 500 guineas, about ten thousand dollars.

"He had never been up in this area because he had a home in the Piedmont area of Virginia. But, after the American Revolution he came up here and built this building."

As Wormley was a Tory I wondered how he could stay in this country. Most of the Tories fled to Canada after the Revolution, or back to England.

"Oh," Brother James said, "the Wormleys were good friends of George Washington, In fact, Washington was at the auction, and, Wormley, because he had never been up here was a bit reluctant to hold on to it. In fact, Washington said, if he didn't want it he would like it himself. Washington had been a surveyor for Lord Fairfax around here and he knew property in this area quite well."

Brother James said that Wormley was a man of wealth and had a large mansion near Urbana, Virginia. That was his home. This was first used as a hunting lodge.

The Wormleys left in 1826 and the property was sold to a Clarke County partnership called Castleman and McCormick. They had it until after the Civil War.

"The McCormicks lived here during the Civil War and after the war the property changed hands several times," Brother James said.

Brother James recounted that there had always been talk of a Civil War near here and "it was thought to be south of here. But then we learned later that the battle was actually here, on the monastery grounds. But, as far as we knew it had never been fully documented.

"With the help of some friends I got some information on the units that were here. But there was still some doubt. It was then that I got a metal detector.

"When I found all of this," Brother James said, pointing to a large glass case filled with Civil War shells, bullets and buckles, "it helped a lot to establish that the battle was here."

As the monastery property has been referred to as Cool Spring the engagement here between Union and Confederate forces on July 18, 1864 is called the Battle at Cool Spring.

"The battle occurred after Confederate General Jubal Early returned to the Shenandoah Valley after an unsuccessful attempt to invade Washington. When he crossed the Shenandoah River at route 7 he had cannons guarding the ford where he had crossed, with two infantry regiments.

"When the Union Army, which had been chasing him, got to the ford they could not cross because of the oppostion. They traveled down the river a ways on the eastern bank and saw that there was another ford across the river that led into what is now the monastery property.

"And so, three thousand Union soldiers came across from the other side and they battled it out for two-and-a-half hours. What happened was that the Union troops were driven back across the river and that was the end of the battle."

"But," he said, "there was a lot of death for two-and-a-half hours."

Total casualties for both sides was 818. the Union had 65 men killed; 301 wounded and 56 missing. The Confederate side had 79 killed; 300 wounded and 17 missing.

Brother James' diligence in pursuit of local Civil War military knowledge has inspired a short, well-written book, published in 1980, on the battle. It is entitled: "The Civil War Engagement at Cool Spring, July 18,1864" by the Rev. Peter J. Meaney, OSB, a Benedictine priest from St. Mary's Abbey, Morristown, N.J.

The Cool Spring battle took place during the eight-day Snickers Gap War. It was one phase of the Shenandoah Valley campaign of 1864.

Father Meaney became interested in the battle when he was traveling through the Shenandoah Valley in the 1970s with a group of students. They were all enthused about the Civil War. They visited Holy Cross Monastery and after Brother James gave them a tour and a "fascinating description" of the battle it "fanned our desire to investigate more thouroughly," Father Meaney said.

The battle brought together some of the famed military men of the Civil War. Northern General Horatio Wright, commanding the Sixth Corps with a force of 25,000 men was pursuing Confederate General Early as he began his retreat from Washington to the Shenandoah Valley on July 12. The pursuit took place, generally, along what is now route 7 and went through such picturesque villages as Hamilton and Purcellville and crossing the Blue Ridge Mountains at Snickers Gap(Bluemont).

On the day before the battle, July 17, General Wright would join forces with Brevett Major General George Crook on a height to the north of Cool Spring Farm, They could look down on the entire scene. General Crook had recently arrived from West Virginia and was the Commander of the Army of West Virginia.

The next day, July 18, the Confederates had cannon and troops guarding the ford where they crossed the river at route 7, so that the Federals could not cross there. However three brigades of infantry and a provisional brigade of dismounted cavalry of the Army of West Virginia under the command of Col. Joseph Thoburn went northward up the river and crossed at an island called Parker's Ford. This crossing led them into the Cool Spring Farm. Some of the soldiers still had to wade chest deep across the Shenandoah to get there. The Parker farm where the Union troops came from was the property of Judge Richard Parker. It was Judge Richard Parker who presided at the John Brown trial in Charlestown, five years earlier.

About three thousand men would eventually cross here. Both sides fought valiantly. But the Northerners, defeated by a superior Confederate force, began the retreat back across the river in the darkness. The details of the battle itself are well outlined in Father Meany's book.

These paragraphs, from the book, sum up the mood of the defeated Northerners:

"As Crook's men came out of the river and ascended the slopes of the Blue Ridge, they certainly did not make a very flattering picture. Wet to the skin and covered with mud from the river banks, they trudged to their camps in sad disarray and equally crestfallen in spirit. The same questions seemed to be on each one's mind. Why didn't the Sixth Corps, which was so near at hand, come across and help us? Why was such a small force ordered across the river and left to face Early's whole Army alone?.......In years to come this engagment would remain a sore spot, somewhat of a mystery, and above all a tragedy they would never forget."

All of these battles would culminate in one great one—the battle of Cedar Creek—on October 1864 in the Shenandoah Valley near Middletown. Many of the great generals would be there: Early and Beauregard for the south; Sheridan, Crook and Custer for the North. And it was at this battle that my great uncle, Pvt. Patrick Long, of the 122nd New York Infantry would participate.

The North would eventually win the day-long battle. The struggle had great significance. It would mark the end of the Southern dominance of the Shenandoah Valley.

Holy Cross Abbey has lived on peacefully, for the most part, for more than forty years. However the quiet, rural life was disturbed as recently as 1989 by, of all things, a golf course.

Across from the monastery land on the east bank of the river is Shenandoah Retreat, a vacation-retirement development. When the property owners bought into the Retreat they were promised that an abandoned golf course on the property would be renovated for their use. The golf course was not developed as planned, and, as time went by Clark County rewrote its laws to prohibit golf courses. However in 1988 a Washington-area developer purchased the golf course and planned to renovate it. The developer said the abandoned land had become an eyesore, a haven for unwanted teen-age drinking parties and other undesirable activities. The renovating of the golf course would bring, they claimed, quieter, more pleasant activity to the east bank. In a hearing to change the zoning laws the attorney for the monks contended that solitude was a way of life for the monks; golf courses have a history of expanding activity when they are built; also, the attorney claimed, when the golf course folded in 1984 the county officials assured the monks that new development there would be contained. Therefore the monks invested more than a million dollars in a new guest house overlooking the river. The guest house, which would be used for retreats for lay people, would face the golf course activity across the river.

"A lot of lay people come here for a quiet day or weekend, away from the stress of urban life to restore their energy in this quiet surrounding. Instead of a quiet opposite shore they would be looking at a golf course," a visitor said.

However, the ruling of the county board, was in favor of the golf course. One of the brothers commented that the golf course would not disturb the monks, as much as it would the lay people who come to the monastery grounds for a short stay for peace and quiet.

Brother James still looks for pre-historic Indian relics and evidence of the Civil War on the monastery grounds.

"After all, he said, "Cool Spring Farm survived the Civil War. I think we will survive this."

- 16 -
THE CLARKS
FROM ALL OVER THE WORLD
TO BLUE MOUNTAIN

Coming to Blue Mountain "just seemed the natural thing to do," Harrell Clark, a native of Bristol, England, and a world traveler, said.

The Clarks reside year-round in the last house designed by Henry de Longfief before he died. It is a rustic-looking beauty, with cedar shingle siding, located off the county road at the juncture of Old Sawmill Road.

"Everybody, all of our friends, think we're bonkers for living up here," Johnny Clark, also a native of England, said.

"But we love it. Somehow it fits us."

The Clark house sits in the forest like it grew there. Both husband and wife are nature lovers and a variety of birds take advantage of the two generous bird feeders nested in the tall trees. The chipmunk squirrels and woodpeckers frolic in front of you as you relax on the front deck taking in nature's wonders.

It is the type of house that stops visitors who catch a look at it as they drive by.

"We will be out here having our afternoon sherry and they will stop the car and just stare," Clark said.

"Well," I said with a laugh, "that's what you get for being so pretty."

The house was chosen to be on the Warren County Historical Society Spring House Tour. The selection gave hundreds of Front Royal and Winchester residents a chance to see Blue Mountain, many of them for the first time.

"I was talking to Bill Brown, the manager of People's Bank in Front Royal. I said, I thought it unusual for the historical society to select our house, a new house, for viewing," Clark said.

"He didn't think it strange at all. He said: 'Blue mountain is now a part of the history of Warren County.'"

The Clarks are part of a large contingent of people from all over the world who have been attracted to Blue Mountain. Mostly weekenders and summer residents, they come from Europe,

South America, and Asia. Many were assigned to the Washington area originally by their governments or their companies.

Dick McCreight, the Clarks neighbor, said the reason for the large contingent of foreign property owners "is that, for many of them, Blue Mountain reminded them of some pleasant, beautiful part of their homeland."

The Clarks were first introduced to Blue Mountain by friends and Capitol Hill neighbors – Harlan and Esta Westover – who have a home on Buck Road.

"First we met Harlan and Esta, and, through them we met the mountain," Johnny said. That was in 1967, she said.

"Those were the best times. We were camping out. They had the shell of their house up. We used to bring the sleeping bags up and put them on the porch," Johnny said.

Clark remembers that there was no water or toilet facilities. Every once in a while someone would start off into the forest.

"We would always say, we are 'going to see Africa,'" Clark said.

They had been visiting the Westovers for several years. One day they were walking near the Westovers when they saw a house that was set back in the forest.

"It didn't exactly have a view. But it had a vista. It was set back enough to have a good look at the trees around it," Johnny said.

"I said to Clark, 'It wouldn't be a bad idea to buy some land. That looks pretty,' pointing to another lot nearby, with a view.

"That's exactly what I thought," Clark said.

"It started with that day," Johnny said.

"We took two years to think about it. We bought the land. But Henry said, 'That's not for you. It's too much off the beaten path.' So eventually we decided on our present location."

The Clarks moved into their new home in March of 1976.

"That first Spring we didn't have any flowers on our land at all. But I spent the whole year cutting down the brush and this year," Johnny said, pointing to a photo album of pictures of flowers, "all of these came up. This Spring was just beautiful.

The pictures showed the wild flowers that bloomed: wild geraniums, daffodils, violets, skull caps, iris and orchids.

"Day after day, week after week, the wild flowers came out. It was quite a show," Clark said with noticeable enthusiasm.

Harrell Clark is one of those resourceful, civilized Britishers who is just as much at home in the Blue Mountain forest as he would be sipping gin and tonic in Singapore, Nairobi, Lagos or any of the other far flung outposts of the former British Empire. He has been to all of those places and many more.

Born in the famed English seaport of Bristol, he must have early on caught the excitement that lures people way from the home fires.

After his school days he joined a London firm as an accountant. One of the clients of the firm "had a string of newspapers in Nigeria" including the <u>West African Pilot</u> in Lagos, the capital.

He went to Nigeria as the general manager of the newspaper chain. He later joined the Nigerian Port Authority in Lagos as the Assistant General Manager of finance. While he was in this position he negotiated a loan with the World Bank for the Port Authority.

He did such good work on this project that the World Bank in Washington offered him a job. In more than twelve years with the World Bank he has surpervised projects in Central and South America, North Africa, Europe, East Africa, West Africa, Australia and other areas of the Far East. He is still employed by the bank as a consultant.

When they first thought of retirement, the Clarks thought of going home to England.

"Our idea was to find a small country town at home, find a house. But at the time we went over there the prices had just sky rocketed."

Johnny joined in humorously:

"Every Colonial, who ever left and worked abroad for England, wants to live in a small country town."

"So," I laughed, "They're all in those small country towns."

"Yes," Johnny laughed, "so a lot of them had to change their minds and a lot of them stayed in the countries they worked in because they couldn't afford to come home. They just retired where they were."

The Clarks look at their Blue Mountain decisions as "something that just fell into place, just happened," as Johnny put it.

"It more or less just happened," Clark said.

"If it hadn't been for the fact the Westovers landed up here and invited us up here, it would never have occurred to us to retire in this country – in the country.

"I like it. In some ways, I suppose, I am more of a country person than Johnny is. Although she has adapted extraordinarily well. But I like it more in the country and I couldn't get out of Washington fast enough.

"Even when the house was being built we said, 'We don't know what it's going to be like. We don't know whether we'll like it. We'll give it a try for three or four years. If we don't feel we shall stick it for the rest of our lives we can always go home'"

Then Johnny joined in:

"We have been here fifteen months and we don't talk about going home any more, we don't talk about moving any more –

"No, we don't," Clark said.

"Well," I said, "This is home, then."

"That's right," Johnny said.

And Clark, looking off in the distance as though he might have been seeing some tall ships arriving at Jamestown in the distant past said:

"I think it is fair enough anyway because Virginia was where the whole thing started and I think it is quite right and proper that we should come back to Virginia."

- 17 -
ON THE TRAIL WITH LEE LIPSCOMB

The Appalachian Trail goes near Lee Lipscomb's Blue Mountain home.
She provides a bench to rest on and hospitality for hikers from all over the country.

"I had a real Indian through here one day with a feather in his cap. He was on his way back to his reservation in North Carolina. He lost the trail. This tickled me, an Indian losing the trail. Why, they made the trail in early days."

Lee Lipscomb was recounting, with gusto, one of her many tales of the Appalachian Trail that winds near her Blue Mountain house. Lee is known from Maine to Georgia (the length of the trail) for her exuberant hospitality to hikers of all ages, sizes and descriptions.

"We even get dogs, too, wearing their little packs, traveling down the trail with the hikers," she said.

The Appalachian Trail is a wilderness footpath stretching 2,015 miles from Springer Mountain in Georgia to Mount Kataliden in Maine. As the trail weaves northward through Virginia it criss-crosses the Skyline Drive and northbound hikers are usually found plodding up route 638 through Blue Mountain. Southbound hikers are coming from Harpers Ferry and cross route 50 at Ashby's Gap on their approach to Blue Mountain. There used to be a continuous path through the forest. However, because of the increase of private land owners, hikers in many areas (like Blue Mountain) are forced to use the roads.

Lee's house is not actually on the trail. She lives on Old Beacon Way, off 638 near the towers. But she might as well be on it. Her warm personality is part of it. Her house is mentioned in Appalachian Trail guidebooks as a good place to "stop for water."

Also, the trail hikers pass on the good news to their fellow travelers. Thus a message like this appears tacked up in a shelter many miles from Blue Mountain: "You can get water at Lipscomb's at Blue Mountain – green mail box, near the Towers."

Lee recalled that one night she was quietly working away in the downstairs part of her home. All of a sudden a voice seemed to come out of nowhere:

"Mrs. Lipscomb?" a young man's voice said. "We've heard your name two hundred and fifty miles away from here on the trail. Could we borrow a broom and sweep out this little house?"

The house referred to is the old metal house that used to house a beacon light on Blue Mountain. (Thus Henry de Longfief's designation of Old Beacon Way.) The house sits on state land a short distance from the Lipscomb property.

"There were four of them," Lee said. "I gave them a broom. They swept out the house and stayed there that night. The next day they brought their clothes down and I put them in the washer and dryer. We had a nice chat and they were on their way. Nice kids."

Lee's been a friend to Appalachian Trail hikers ever since 1971 when she and her late husband, Granville Lipscomb and their children moved to Blue Mountain as permanent residents.

"I've got the nicest letters from people from all over," she said.

"Some people don't want to give hikers water. Maybe they've had unfortunate experiences. I haven't. I haven't had a single bad experience. And I find thank you notes in the mailbox. On the car windshield. It's a nice feeling."

Lee Lipscomb wears the world like a loose garments. A blythe spirit, outgoing, trusting, as happy as one of the blue jays singing in her garden.

Born in Nashville, Tennessee she proudly recalls that she graduated in the same high school class as Dinah Shore. The setting for the graduation was quite impressive too: the stage of the Grand Old Opry.

Her future husband, Granville Lipscomb, was her neighbor. At the age of 24 he received his doctorate in analytical chemisty.

"He was, at that time, the youngest person to receive his doctorate in the subject," she said.

The brilliant young chemist had quite a career ahead of him. He eventually became the chief chemist for the Food and Drug Administration in Washington. He was in charge of all of the FDA laboratories in the nation.

The Lipscombs had three children: David, now with the Canadian government, Karen of Arlington and Robert, an attorney with a Los Angeles law firm.

As the years progressed, Lee recalls, she and her husband were thinking about places to retire, although his retirement was still several years off. They had traveled a lot and they liked Virginia, especially the Roanoke area. They were living in Arlington at the time.

"Then one Sunday," she said, "we saw this ad in the paper for Blue Mountain. We decided to go see it." The year was 1966.

"Well," she said, "we were very much impressed right away. We liked it. Henry (de Longfief) was not a hard sell. But he made you feel about Blue Mountain the way he did."

The Lipscomb didn't decide right away. They continued to look around.

"One place we looked at had some beautiful views. But they had cut down all the trees. Trees are part of the woods. They <u>are</u>the woods," she said.

Finally, in 1969, they decided on Blue Mountain.

"We had been planning on building a house in Arlington. Then we started to think: 'This is where we really want to live. Let's build a house here'"

Lee remembers that "Henry and Granville worked on the design of the house together."

"When Granville would suggest something that Henry thought was not necessary Henry would say 'that's too expensive,' Granville would have to keep saying to him, 'Henry, that's what I want,'" Lee recalled.

The Lipscomb house is one of the more substantial homes of Blue Mountain. It has the style of a great mountain lodge with all of the comfort of a home in the city. A large fireplace is the focus of the living room that has a 20 foot ceiling. Great picture windows bring in the natural beauty of the surrounding forest. The landscaped gardens are outstanding.

"This house was fun to build," Lee said. "When it was going up we would rush through dinner in Arlington, drive out here to look at the 'hole in the ground' and then back to Arlington before midnight."

Shortly before the Lipscomb dream house was finished part of the dream was shattered. On the way from Dulles airport to Blue Mountain in March of 1971, Granville Lipscomb was killed in an auto accident. Lee was taken to the hospital seriously injured.

"It happened so fast and with such an awful impact that I don't remember what happened at all. I was in a coma for several days. When I came out of it they told me Granville had died. Thank God I don't remember. It would be too much," she said.

Dr. Lipscomb, who was in charge of the FDA pesticide program at the time, was coming from a pesticide conference in Kansas City. Lee had traveled from Blue Mountain to Dulles to meet his plane. On the way back to Blue Mountain, on route 55, near a thorofare, they were waiting behind a car that was making a left turn.

"We were hit by one of those enormous milk tank trucks, traveling east, so I am told. I don't remember anything," she said.

After the accident, after her injured arm healed, Lee slowly put her life back together. She decided to live at Blue Mountain. Robert, her youngest son, had been living at Blue Mountain when the accident occurred. He finished high school in Front Royal and graduated in June of 1971. Karen, her daughter, lives in Arlington, and visits on weekends.

Granville and Lee Lipscomb liked a lot of company. That's why they built such a big house at Blue Mountain.

"We have lots of space, because we like lots of company. And I do have lots of company now. We were just going to enjoy life. But things don't always turn out the way you think they are going to. There's not much you can do about that," she said.

Looking out at the broad vistas and the trees and flowers that surround her house she said:

"But it is heavenly up here. It is really beautiful.

"People ask me if I don't get lonesome. I really haven't. I've got too much to do. I've never been bored. I don't know how people get bored, really. I honest to goodness don't understand."

How does she spend her time? Does she get involved in activities in Blue Mountain or Front Royal?

"Now listen," she says firmly, like a real Blue Mountaineer, "I don't join these organizations. I came up here to get away from all that. Who needs it. I mainly work on my house. I love to take walks in the forest. I visit. I have a lot of company. I always figure what I don't get done today, maybe I'll get it done tomorrow. Maybe it won't ever get done. But who knows. I'm not going to knock myself out. But I go, I travel an awful lot. My daughter Karen and I had a wonderful trip to Colombia. We were way up in the Andes, living with the people. And I travel a lot around here."

She has a good vehicle, an International Scout, for the winding dirt roads of Blue Mountain.

"It's great to drive all of the time, but especially in the winter when the roads get icy up here," she said.

She likes the Blue Mountain people.

"It is a small friendly place. Everybody helps each other. There are children growing up, up here. And that's nice. We get together from time to time. We have parties. But we have our privacy, too. None of us are living in each other's pockets here. It's a nice balance of sociability and privacy."

The people "on the Trail" are a big part of her Blue Mountain life too.

One day as many as fifteen people stopped by to get water, rest, or pass the time of day. The average days see three or four people stop.

"They are all ages," she said. "You would be surprised at how many lone women you see on the trail.

"There was one woman, up on the road, she didn't stop. She was 77 years old. She was from Quebec. She had a full pack on. She didn't speak a bit of English.

"A man who had met her told me about her. 'She's really determined,' he said. 'She says he's going to make it to Maine.'"

"One woman stopped once," he said. "She was from California and had started out on the trail in Georgia. She had broken her arm badly. She had to go to the hospital. After she got out of the hospital she got right back on the trail. Her daughter from California joined her. She fell and hurt her shoulder. When she got here I told her I had a sling for her arm. She said the doctor told her she couldn't use a sling. She stayed and talked for an hour. She was going to a hospital in Baltimore for a check up. Her daughter was going to take her and then return her back to the exact spot on the trail. She wasn't going to miss one bit of it."

One young fellow, who started out in Georgia, stopped and while they were talking, said:

"I've got a deadline. I've got to finish in Maine by August 1st."

"Well," Lee said, "you better not stay here talkin', you better get going." They both laughed.

Lee Lipscomb was part of the "Agnes McDonald Bear Story" previously related.

"When Agnes called that night and said there was a bear I got in my car and went down. By the time I got there he was gone.

"The next night Agnes called and said 'he's back' so we rushed down again. This time we saw him. We were in the car. He started walking toward the car. I backed away. He looked mighty big to me. He was standing on his hind legs."

She recalls that later on she got some "bear advice" from a man who had hunted near the Blue Mountain area for 35 years. (Hunting is not allowed at Blue Mountain.)

"He told me that if you see a bear and you are on foot to run downhill. Their front legs, he said, are shorter than hind legs. If they run downhill they get off balance and fall over. So, he said, they rarely run downhill. They can run uphill better than downhill.

"I told him if I saw a bear, and I was on foot, I'd probably just faint and he'd walk over me. I wouldn't be able to think which way to run," she laughed.

Lee's enthusiasm about Blue Mountain is infectious, and, in a way, self-defeating. She has been thinking about buying the lot next to her for several years. Her neighbor, who owns the lot said to her one day:

"Before we came out here we are thinking about selling. Then we came here and we talk to you and we change our mind about selling. You make it sound so good."

One of Lee's best "trail stories" is about a boy who had been on the trail all day and stopped by to get water.

"He was pretty tired and he said he would like to go to a motel in Front Royal for the night and clean up and rest up. I took him down to Front Royal. We went to five motels before we found one that he liked and could afford. So I bid him good bye and went back to Blue Mountain. When I got back on the mountain I got a phone call from him. He said:

'I had a stick with me and I think I left it in your car. It's just a plain old stick. But you know I've had that stick ever since I started out.'

"I told him I would see that he got the stick. I said I would put the stick in the phone booth at Linden – that's where he was going to pick up the trail the next morning.

"So I went down and I put a note on the stick and it said, 'If your name is not Jimmy don't touch this stick'"

"Well, at Christmas time I got a box of the most delicious home made cookies and a beautiful thank you note from him."

- 18 -
MOSBY'S RANGERS AND BLUE MOUNTAIN

"The cavalry-camp lies on the slope

Of what was late a vernal hill

But now like a pavement bare-

An outpost in the perilous wilds

Whichever the lone and still

But Mosby's men are there

Of Mosby best beware."

- Herman Melville, 1866

Blue Moutain was a John Singleton Mosby "outpost in the perilous wilds" according to Front Royal historian Lola Wood.

"After their raids, that's where they went, that's where they hid out, on Blue Mountain," said Mrs. Wood who is a granddaughter of a Mosby Ranger. Mosby was the South's most famous guerilla fighter in the Civil War. His roving band of 800 horsemen struck fear, and a lot of embarrassment, into the hearts of much larger Union contingents.

Mosby was a tough fighter, using behind the lines, guerilla-like tactics to harass his Yankee enemy.

"Mosby had no headquarters, "Mrs. Wood said. "That was his strength. Mosby had rangers living all around here. And his men would visit these homes in the Virginia countryside and they were always welcome.

"Mount Bleak and Belle Grove are examples of homes where Mosby visited and his men were entertained," she said.

Both of these homes are a short distance from Blue Mountain, near Paris. Mount Bleak is part of Skyland State Park and is open to visitors at various times during the year.

Mrs. Wood said that what was known as the Mosby Confederacy was bounded by Linden, the Blue Ridge mountains (Blue Mountain) and Snickers' Gap (Bluemont) on the west; then to

Middleburg to Marshall and back to Linden. They would make attacks outside of this area but the Confederacy was where they would spend their nights and good bit of their time," she said. (It should be noted that during the Civil War years several of the communities mentioned in this chapter had different names, e.g.: Rectors (crossroads is now Atoka; Piedmont is Delaplane; Salem is Marshall and Snickerville is Bluemont."

Lola Wood as born February 17, 1906 in a beautiful rural area south of Front Royal, off route 522, that bears the musical name: Harmony Hollow. "It was just wonderful growing up there. We were surrounded by apple and peach orchards," she said.

In 1910, however, the United States government bought a large tract of land to the east which also included a large portion of Harmony Hollow. That land extended from a section now on route 55, across route 522 and up into a large area in Harmony Hollow.

"On that site they created the largest cavalry horse breeding station in the United States," she said.

(The property is still owned by the United States but the majority of the land is now occupied by the National Zoo which breeds endangered species of animals from all over the world.) Animals, including the exotic African deer, roam the hillside, much to the wonderment of passing motorists. Also in Harmony Hollow is the U.S. Customs. Dogs are trained here to scent out drugs. Nations from all over the world send their enforcement officers there to learn the U.S. anti-drug tactics with the use of dogs.

In 1930 the Federal Government purchased more land, including acreage in Harmony Hollow. This land became part of the Shenandoah National Forest. "Harmony Hollow is now completely surrounded by government land," she said. Like Front Royal well-driller Larry LeHew, Mrs. Wood descends from the pioneer person of Front Royal: Peter LeHew, the founder of LeHewTown, now Front Royal. Peter LeHew was an English agent representing the Crown on the Lord Fairfax Proprietary Survey.

"My maternal great-great-grandmother was a LeHew. She was the daughter of Spencer LeHew, who was the son of Peter LeHew. "Spencer LeHew owned a large plantation and also a tavern in Front Royal," she said.

Reflecting on Harmony Hollow, she said:

"I grew up out there in the country until I was about fourteen years old. Everybody had to do more than one thing.

Besides growing fruit we raised cattle, hogs and sheep and we had to have horses to work the farm.

My father was a farmer and a merchant in Harmony Hollow. He was also the postmaster for the little community of Arco, in Harmony Hollow." One of her biggest thrills as a little girl was to actually see Colonel Mosby.

"My uncle George, lived near Masanutta Springs in Rockingham County. I would visit him there when I was a little girl. I was four years old the summer I saw Colonel Mosby. "Colonel Mosby would spend the summer at Masanutta Springs. He would pass by my uncle George's house every day, on his horse, on his way into Harrisonburg. One day, when he saw Mosby approaching my uncle took my hand and said he wanted me to meet the famous Colonel Mosby.

"I went out to see Mosby. But I remember his horse more. There was a light saddle and blanket on the horse. The horse kept prancing so much I was afraid he was going to step on me. I was so scared of the horse I never did get a good look at Mosby.

Her grandfather was John Alexander Silman and her great uncle was James Albert Silman. They both enlisted in Company F, 43rd Battalion, Mosby's Rangers, in Front Royal. She said there was a lot of entertaining during the War. "The Rangers would visit and have parties at such places as Mount Bleak and Belle Grove. They would usually be there at mealtime."

"A lot of people don't realize that the Mosby Rangers were a battalion, they were a regular part of the Southern Army. They weren't off by themselves, they were part of the Army," she said. Her grandfather died in 1880 as the result of a spinal injury received in a Civil War skirmish.

"At night they would head back to Blue Mountain, which is the main part of Mosby's Confederacy. In the winter time they would build crude huts on Blue Mountain, so they could have a fire to keep warm. "They would rendezvous, a lot of times at Atoka, which was called Rector's Crossroads. They would make their battle plans, then, after the battle, they would head back to the mountains.

In later years, after the war, one of the rangers, Tom Sealock ran a boarding house near Freezeland Orchard, on the road to Blue Mountain. "Mosby kept in touch with him. In fact, Mosby's daughter would come out to spend the summer at the Sealock house," Mrs. Wood said.

"Belle Grove" and "Mount Bleak" the two great homes mentioned by Mrs. Wood are till standing, only a short distance from Blue Mountain, near Paris. They were both considered "Mosby homes" and their doors were always open to Mosby men and the homes were centers of entertainment during the War. Much of the information that follows is from the "Journals of Amanda Virginia Edmonds: Lass of the Mosby Confederacy- 1859-1867." Her son, Benjamin Curtis Chappelear inherited the journals and gave them to Nancy Chappelear Baird to edit. Miss Edmonds nickname was "Tee."

In her introduction to the Journals, Mrs. Baird writes: "The Mosby men stayed in homes of the local residents rather than in regular army camps, so 'Belle Grove' was rather like a perpetual house party during this period. 'Tee' in her mid twenties was quite spirited, restless, romantic and a love of excitement and was in her element at this time."

Belle Grove fulfilled much of the "Gone With the Wind" atmosphere of the Civil War. It was a beautiful Southern mansion. It had lovely women whose hearts were torn by the fact that their men were all off fighting the war in far off places. These men were usually in the cavalry, the most dashing and romantic aspect of 19th Century military life. And these men were riding with and under the command of such authentic Southern heroes as: General J.E. B. Stuart, Turner Ashby and, of course, John Singleton Mosby. If it had all this romance, Belle Grove also had Negro slaves and all the problems that slavery brought to the South.

"We have insight into the relationship between slave and owner not often presented," Mrs. Baird writes, "which lasted throughout their lives. The early war years came upon the heels of the burning of crops on a nearby farm by the slaves when their owner was away for some days in Warrenton on business and the trial and execution of John Brown.

"Tee's favorite first cousin, Tommy Settle (son of Abner Settle, owner of nearby Mount Bleak) was an uncle was one of the Fauquier Militia guarding Brown during the trial." The depth of feeling of the young Amanda (and much of the South) toward Brown is revealed in this journal entry on Dec. 2, 1859, the day Brown was hung at Charles Town:

"This day will long, long be remembered, as the one that witnessed old Brown-the murderer, robber and destroyer of our Virgin peace—swinging from the gallows. O! how many are rejoicing at his end."

The next lines, however, reveal the fear in the slave-owning Virginia countryside of an invasion by more abolitionists like Brown:

"There are many that do not retire tonight or last night in fear of the vile enemy. I fear no danger. They are not honest enough to come while we are prepared to fight them. No, they had rather defer their trip on this soil, when they think we least suspect. O! vile, inhuman race, may God ever protect us from your bloodthirsty fool hardy hands.

Belle Grove was built in 1812 by Isaac Settle. Earlier, in 1808 Isaac Settle bought the nearby Mount Bleak property. There was already a house on the property owned by George Edmonds. Isaac Settle built the main portion of the Mount Bleak house apparently when his son Abner Settle married in 1835. At the time of Amanda's journals (1859-1867) Abner Settle and his children were living at Mount Bleak. Amanda's mother, Elizabeth Settle Edmonds, was a sister of Abner Settle. Abner was Amanda's uncle. This genealogy is important because it shows the closeness of the families in this area, many of whom were related to each other. Slavery played a part when Amanda's father Lewis Edmonds died in 1857. "With the death of Lewis Edmonds, Belle Grove and the slaves and personal property had to be put up to settle his debts," Mrs. Baird writes. "These had chiefly been brought on by his kindness in signing notes for his friends, which they did not make good. This caused him to have to mortgage Belle Grove."

On the day of the sale, Nov. 3, 1857, Amanda has this entry:

"A large number of persons to the sale.....When I saw Pa's saddle going I could not refrain from shedding tears. O! I think they ought to have kept it and his riding horse (Billy) which was sold to Mr. Rogers for fifty dollars..." In commenting on the long-range effect of the auction Mrs. Baird said: " The public did not bid against the Edmonds family, so they were able to buy "Belle Grove" at the auction apparently via a mortgage extension. They seem to have borrowed more money during the war or the interest had accumulated so that something had to be done or they would lose "Belle Grove." The solution was for Aunt Tee to be the sacrificial lamb in that her mother made her marry Uncle Armistead Chappelear who was in love with her although she was apparently not with him. He sold the farm that his father had given him to pay off the mortgage on "Belle Grove" which gave her family a home for life."

Most of the subject matter in the journals from 1857 to 1860 seems to be filled with the monotony of every day life. However, as the war begins in 1861 the journals pick up to a spirited pace to match the feverish activity going on in the Piedmont Valley.

As Virginia was the battleground for most of the war this intensity is understandable. Paris, Blue Mountain and the Piedmont were in the center of furious military activity. Nearby Ashby Gap was one of those breaks in the Blue Ridge Mountains where troops of both sides poured through for battles close to Washington (life Bull Run) or going the other way to the Shenandoah Valley where Stonewall Jackson was fighting great land battles. Several entries from March of 1863 give the flavor of the excitement of not knowing whether a friendly Rebel or a detested Yank would come to the door:

"March 3: A report that the Yanks camped near last night; so I though it best to return home, it being safer for the horses, too. Oh! such a delightful ride on a captured Yank pony.....

"March 8: What a way to spend the Sabbath, the weather so disagreeable that we could not go to church. We spend the day in various ways. Oh! we had such a treat yesterday, seven or eight rebels in a squad. We were sitting in the window, doing justice to a jar of brandy grapes, which drew from them a smile and a bow.

March 21: Yank prisoners walking up this evening. Capt. Mosby captured and paroled them. They looked quite humble, dismounted and on their way back to Yankeedom.

"April 8: To our pleasant surprise we have John Gibson and two other Rebels dine with us. They came for meat. Fifteen more are here in the yard.....Cousin Sandy, Mr. Buck and Mr. Cloud came after dark, members of the 7th Reg. under Col. Dulany. They are now in the neighborhood. Oh, it makes a body feel different when our soldiers are about. I fear our happiness will be short lived for we know or fear they will not tarry with us long. One good deed done with their coming, breaking up the distilleries."

(The Col. Dulany mentioned here is the same Col. Richard Dulany who, in 1906, sold the land that was later to become Freezeland Orchard (next to Blue Mountain) to the Crawford and White families. See chapter on Freezeland, the Great Orchard.)

"April 18: Heavy cannoning in the Valley. I really felt so bad, that I kept close to the house and didn't go out to hear a single boom. A call from Mit and Bell, as they returned from Paris. I was mounted on the wood pile talking with them on their horses, when our attention was arrested by two soldiers riding up. The girls went on and they put up for the night. They introduced themselves as Judge's Tyler's and John Hill Carter's sons........They retired soon after, pleading fatigue and loss of rest."

"April 20: In spite of rain had two nice Rebels to dinner. Capt. Gaither and Shelby of Maryland, members of 1st Reg., some of the wealthiest men in Maryland. No end of this tongue, quite interesting and gave us an account of a skirmish he had with the Yanks last week. How I do love to see strangers and hear them talk of their adventures and everything connected with our

Mosby Ranger John Alexander Silman used to hide out on Blue Mountain in between sporadic raids behind the Union line. He is the grandfather of Front Royal historian Mrs. Lola Wood.

Commanding officer that on March 17 he had attacked "a body of the enemy's Cavalry at Herndon Station, in Fairfax County, completely routing the. I brought off 25 prisoners.")

Lola Wood, Front Royal Historian and granddaughter of a Mosby Ranger,
tells about the Rangers hideaway on Blue Mountain.

But, danger was always present in this area, as reflected in this entry for April 28, 1863:

"After putting aside the dissipation of the evening, and having retired about an hour, I was suddenly awakened by someone calling Jack. I immediately bounded to my sorrow heard the vile Yanks were marching up in force. They have gotten as far as Upperville.

"We had our soldiers aroused from their sweet slumber. Oh! I disliked to see them awakened, for they hadn't more than gotten to sleep in good fashion. They soon dressed, had their horses saddled and kept watch the rest of the night. I don't know when I have been so agitated or unnerved."

As Mrs. Woods states, Blue Mountian and the surrounding mountain areas were areas of safety and refuge for Mosby's Rangers and other Southern soldiers. The entry of Feb. 6 mentions that "we spend a pleasant day until the rumor came that the Yanks were in Upperville......Four of them (Rebels) leave for safer shelter in the mountains, the remaining four spend the night with us."

As a Civil War buff I have read several "diary" books, usually written by Southern women. I can only say that I found the "Journals of Amanda Virginia Edmonds" exceedingly interesting and one of the best diaries I have ever read. It gives real insight into those times. Mrs. Baird is to be highly complimented for her excellent and painstaking job of bringing them to publication so that they may be enjoyed, not only by buffs like myself, but by scholars and historians, too.

Any visitor to the home of Mrs. Wood in Front Royal today can sense they are surrounded by memories of the South in the Civil War. The presence of her fondly remembered grandfather is intact, even tho he is deceased. I was reminded of this when I paid her a visit and, while coming up the walk noticed a tombstone in a carton on the front lawn.

"That's not my tombstone," she laughed, as she welcomed me.

The gravestone, I learned, was part of a project of the United Daughters of the Confederacy, to make sure that every Confederate veteran in this area has a proper stone on his gravesite.

"I am waiting for someone in the family to come and pick it up," she said. It was a vivid reminder, to me, of the reverence and affection the South, and ladies like Mrs. Wood, will always have for their fallen heroes.

Earl Baltimore grew up in Little Africa, the mountain community that was founded by former slaves on nearby Rattlesnake Mountain.

- 19 -
The Road to Little Africa

The road to Little Africa is a, journey back in time. It leads to a haunted, hunted and fearful America of the 1850s when escaped slaves from Virginia plantations sought freedom on the tops of mountains.

Little Africa is the name of a once all-black farming community on Rattlesnake Mountain. Rattlesnake, just over the line in Fauquier County, is the mountain only a few miles southeast of Blue Mountain. The two mountains are connected by route 638.

Blue Mountain and Rattlesnake Mountain have one thing in common: their first inhabitants, in the mid 1850s, were escaped slaves. The late Charlie Reynolds of Howellsville, my old, black friend was the first to tell me of the former slaves of Blue Mountain.

"Why they even built two churches on Blue Mountain," Charlie said. One of the churches was destroyed by fire. The other structure is still standing on 638 about a mile up the road from Charlie's place. It has been converted into a home.

There is a significant difference, however, between the blacks on the two mountains. Very little is known about the Blue Mountain community and no descendants could be found to trace their roots back there.

This is not so of Little Africa. Hundreds of black people, living today, all over Virginia, Maryland and the Washington area can trace their beginnings back to Little Africa. And many of them come back here, on a regular basis, twice a month. The main force that links them all together is Mount Paran Baptist Church, a pretty, white-painted church, vibrantly alive today at Little Africa.

Mrs. Brenda McLee of Front Royal, the church historian, says the church was founded before 1877. However no exact date has, as yet, been determined. The church boats that it has been serving the Little Africa community for more than 114 years---(from before 1877 to the present writing---1991).

I was a guest of the church on Mother's Day, May 12, 1991. It was a wonderful experience to attend the service and, later, to talk to several members of the congregation, many of whom went to Cherry Hill School at Little Africa. The little one-room schoolhouse, part of America's segregated past, was opened in 1898 and closed in 1951. The building still stands at Little Africa today. It has been converted to a private residence.

On that Mother's Day I was introduced to descendents who bore all the old names of Little Africa—names that extended back to the actual beginning of the community: Baltimores, Jacksons, Crisemons, Fords, Combs and others. There were more than 60 in the congregation that morning and they keep coming back , every second and fourth Sunday. The pastor is the Rev. Henry Ausberry.

I was profoundly impressed by what happened here. This is a tiny part of Virginia on top of a Blue Ridge mountain. It is difficult to find on any map. In the 1850s some brave, but I am sure fearful, too, blacks climbed their way to freedom on top of this mountain. After the Civil War they wre legally free. They could have left here. Communities as fragile as this, white and black, have disappeared—gone with the wind—all over America. But, they apparently liked what they found here. They started a farming community. They built a church. Later, a school. Today their descendants come back here, sometimes a hundred or more at a time, to worship in the church their ancestors built more than hundred years ago. I felt, as I walked around Little Africa, I was moving on sacred ground.

Thankfully I located two people that could tell me the story of how it was to grow up on Little Africa many years ago.

Earl Baltimore,66, lives in Front Royal today. I met him in May of 1991 when he was mowing the grass around Mount Paran Chruch.

Mrs.Sylvia Jackson Gaskins of McLean,Virginia, one of the daughters of the legendary late Guy Jackson of Little Africa, helped me with the interesting details of her father's life.

Earl Baltimore's great-grandfather, Dayton Baltimore, on his mother's side was a slave. But his first firm visual image of slavery as a child rested in his great-grandfather Ginny Combs.

"She was an old woman, a real old woman," Earl said. She was a slave,she died up here on Little Africa when she was one hundred and seventeen years old. I remember her sitting under a tree, to get the shade. She wore long dresses and a bonnet."

"She went to church," Earl said, pointing to Mount Paran Church. "But my father and mother they would go to the church in Markham. This church,Mount Paran, is called the 'old school'. They belonged to the 'new school'".

Earl Baltimore is one of the 14 children of Stanley Hubert and Virginia Daugherty Baltimore. His father was born in 1898 and died in 1969. His mother was born in 1903. She died in 1986. Her family was from West Virginia.

Earl Baltimore is indebted to his relative Welbert L. Baltimore for the following information that traces the roots of the Baltimore family on Little Africa. Wilbert Baltimore presented this information at the Baltimore family reunion on August 12, 1989 in Front Royal.

(To explain it in a more simplified manner I will trace back from Earl Baltimore.)

Earl Baltimore's great-grandfather (on his father's side) was Peter Baltimore, Sr. He was born in 1823 and died in 1884. His wife was Alsy Baltimore who was born 1830 and, according to one report, died in 1933. Different death dates were given for Alsy Baltimore. She could have been 99 or 103 years old when she died.

Peter Baltimore Sr.'s son, Peter Baltimore, Jr., (Earl's grandfather) was born in 1858 and died in 1932. He married Lucy Jackson Baltimore. She was born in 1861 and died in 1927. They had eleven children, including Stanly Hubert, Earl's father, who was born in 1898.

Peter Baltimore, Jr., Earl's grandfather is the key name in the genealogy because the Little Africa land was conveyed to him on Oct. 21, 1874.

Before the mountain was called Rattlesnake or Little Africa it was called Marshall Mountain, after the famous Marshall family of Fauquier County, which included John Marshall, fourth Chief Justice of the U.S. Supreme Court.

"In the conversations down through the years," Wilbert Baltimore writes, "the Baltimore property belonged to Peter Baltimore, the son of Alsy Baltimore. In researching the deed…..the property was conveyed to Peter M. Baltimore and George Miles from property of the Marshall Mountain Farm by Harrison Robertson.

"Harrison Robertson, a lawyer, was the husband of the daughter (son-in-law) of Dr. Jacqueline Marshall, who was the heir of the Mountain Farm after her father's death." The land consisted of 56 acres and the purchase price of $672.00.

On Jan. 5,1880 the land was separated equally between Peter Baltimore, Jr. and George Miles.

Wilbert Baltimore did extensive research at the National Archives in Washington, D.C., the Fauquier County Courthouse in Warrenton and other sources to gain his information. He noted that in his survey of the various census the categories of race were: white, black, mulatto, Hispanic and Indian.

"The entire family was listed as mulattoes," Wilbert Baltimore wrote.

If Mount Paran Church was unifying force at Little Africa, then the little one-room school house, Cherry Hill School, also played a significant role. Everyone I talked to seemed to have happy memories of the little school even tho some of them trudged more than five miles, each way, up and down the mountain for their education.

"I'll never forget those days. They were happy days," Earl said. "I lived down by Linden, which was more than a two mile walk up the mountain. I started to go to school when I was seven years old. Papa went to Markham and bought me a tablet, and a pencil and brand new shoes and a dinner bucket. I had a little tin bucket to carry my lunch in.

"I used to have a rhyme I would say when I was a little boy:

'Earl Baltimore is my name,

Linden is my station,

I go to school at Cherry Hill,

To get my education.'

"It was just a little school. My teacher was Ruby Hunter. My father and mother went to the same school. Mose Jeffers was their teacher."

Earl lived near Belle Mead, which is were route 55 meets route 726, or as it is known on the map: "Little Africa Rd."

"I walked up every morning to the school. We would stop at Guy Jackson's spring and get water. We would have two buckets to carry the water. Everyone brought their own glass and their own towel. The glass was to drink from and the towel to wash your hands. I had a lot of fun in this school.

"There were seven grades. It was an all-black school. You had to remember that this was a time of segregation. Black schools and white schools. Miss Jesse, she was the superintendent. She was black. She came up every three months to see how we was doing.

"We had a big pot bellied stove set in the middle of the floor. Whoever acted bad, they would have to go out and chop wood for the stove," Earl said.

Mrs. Edna Ford Kurtz, who came all the way from California for the Mother's Day service, remembers some of the happiest times were in the wintertime, when it would snow.

"All boys had sleds. So we would walk up in the snow. But then we would have a sleigh ride down. That was great fun," she said. She was born in 1920 in Ford's Hollow, a few miles from Little Africa.

Mrs. Mary Ford, 93, was the oldest mother at the service. She is Mrs. Kurtz' mother and was born in Ford's Hollow in 1898. She went to Cherry Hill School around 1905, she remembers, and Mr. Jeffers was her teacher.

Mrs. Helen Ford McLee, mother of the church historian Brenda McLee and cousin of Mrs. Jurtz, was born in 1931 and remembers a five mile walk every day to school, "a real walk in the winter," she said.

Earl's father, Stanley Baltimore, was a farmer at Little Africa for several years.

"At one time there was nothing but black farmers up here. That's why they called it 'Little Africa,'" Earl said.

Besides his father, Earl remembers Guy Jackson, his uncle Tommy Baltimore, Mose Monroe, Will Dayton and others as farmers. Most of them had large families like the Baltimores and Jacksons.

"After my father got married he left Little Africa and moved down the road near Linden," Earl said.

Of the fourteen Baltimore children, eight were girls and six were boys. The family has spread all over the East and the South with members in Harrisburg, Pa., Baltimore, New York City, Washington,D.C. and Texas. But Earl stayed "home." Or, at least, close to Little Africa. He and his wife live in Front Royal.

He has a regular job at the IGA grocery store in Marshall. He even works on his day off cutting lawns with his high-powered mowing equipment. He is very proud of the small Baltimore family cemetery on Little Africa. He keeps it in immaculate condition.

The first time I met him he took me right to the cementery and started pointing to the graves of his relatives:

"Uncle Tommy Baltimore is buried there—his wife Ginny is next to him—there's grandfather Peter Baltimore and there is the grave of my mother and father."

I was introduced to Earl by author Nancy Chappelear Baird of Delaplane. Mrs. Baird is working on a new book about the more than 200 family cemeteries in Fauquier County.

"I've always been impressed at how well-kept this small cemetery is, thanks to the care given to it by Earl. It certainly makes my job easier. The stones are easy to read," she said.

Earl said that when he wasn't going to school and the other children helped their father with his farm work.

He described a system of farming—share-cropping or tenant farming—that has been common in the South since after the Civil War.

The war devastated the famlands and the economy of the south. Although the former slaves were now free, they had to get used to a whole system of economic life that put them on their own, to earn a living the best way they could. On the other hand, the white landholder was left with a lot of land, but no one to work it.

This is when share-cropping came into existence. The black farmers agreed to work the land in return for a portion of the land that would be theirs which they could feed their families and also sell some of the fruits of their labor at the local market.

The white landowner, in most cases, agreed to provide housing for the black families and to take care of them financially until the first crop came in. In return the landowner got part of his own vacant land farmed and made productive.

"My father," Earl said, "farmed for a man named Will Smith. Mr. Smith owned the land.

"We farmed a third of the land. We got two and he got one. That means that if we grew sixty bushel of potatoes, we got forty bushel and he got twenty. "Papa worked for years for twenty dollars a month. They called it 'working' by the year.' You get a place to live on the farm, and grow your own food and sell some and feed his cows and feed his chickens.

"Papa raised fourteen children like that," Earl said.

Mrs. Sylvia Jackson Gaskins, a daughter of the late Guy Jackson, said that her father told her he was taken to Little Africa by his parents in 1902 when he was four years old. He was one of 13 Jackson children brought up on Little Africa at the turn of the century. He spent most of his life on the mountain as a farmer. They had five daughters, including Mrs. Gaskins.

Mrs. Gaskins' daughter, Courtney, when she was in high school in 1983 wrote a very perceptive, short history of her family and their rise from slavery to the present day world. It is entitled: "The Educational Tradition: the Story of a Black Virginian's Family." She has allowed me to quote from it.

Her great-grandfather Albert Dowl was a servant slave at the U.S. Naval Academy at Annapolis.

"Many Southern cadets of the United States Naval Academy," she writes,"kept in their possession male salves as valets. Albert Dowl, my mother's great grandfather was a servant slave at Annapolis, where he was allowed to obtain an education. He is blieved to have been taught secretly by cadets who sympathized with his plight.

"After the Civil War he gained his feedom and settled somewhere in Fauquier County, near Markham, Virginia. There he married and raised one child, Amanda, teaching both his wife and child to read and write. He also gave lessons to some of the neighboring children, who were too young to walk the long distance to the nearest school."

She offers an interesting insight into the problems of black and white women having children in rural Virginia, many times when there was no doctor available:

"There were certain trades that free black men and women learned from the experience of slavery. Midwfiery was one such occupation practiced by women who were former slaves and learned through generations of teachings. Two of my great grandparents were taught midwifery. Thomas' wife, Ida Jackson, was taught to read and write by a white woman she worked for. Moreover she midwifed babies of black women who lived in the community.

Likewise Amanda Dowl, the daughter of Albert and my mother's grandmother, secured her instructions in midwifery from the same midwife who helped in her own birth. Amanda delivered many children of unmarried white and black young women. She was told many times to keep the babies when the parents of the young girls refused to accept the children because of their illegitimacy.

"Amanda taught these children to read and write as well as her own. However she was later told that it wasn't right for a black women to raise white children and she was forced to find homes for them or sent them to orphanages."

She also writes about the Cherry Hill School:

"The sons of many former slaves were educated in one-room school houses and churches. Some only went so far as the sixth grade in their education because they were forced to quit school to get jobs in order to help support the family. My mother's father, Guy Jackson, was one of the thirteen children, none of whomever graduated from high school.

"Guy went to a school with one teacher and sixty children who were of a variety of ages and grade levels…Later, he married and raised five daughters. All of these children went to the same one room school house that their father attended; but the school was not improved to a point where there were two teachers."

Courtney's father, Louis Gaskins, and his brothers and sisters "walked over five miles to the closest school wich has two room and two teachers. Upon finishing elementary school, he was bussed to Manassas, an hour-and-a-half each way, because that was the closest school where blacks were permitted to attend." After her father reached 11th grade he had to drop out because his father was dying of cancer. Her father served in the Navy and in World War II.

"His experience in the armed forces made it easier to find a job when the war was over. Taking odd jobs my father made enough money to start a family. He married my mother, Sylvia Johnson and they had five children.

"Even though he never completed high school, my father was able to secure a job in the postal service, where he has been working for over thirty years."

Courtney Gaskins, who can look back at more than 140 years of American history in her own family, contrasts the various generations as she writes:

"Today's education for the black American has improved a great deal since my great-great-grandfather's time. The schools of my ancestors' time have grown from a one-room schoolhouses where children of different ages and grade levels are taught by one or two teachers, to an institution that holds over four thousand, all classified by their ability to perform in a classroom.

"It has changed to a classroom that contains both black and white, each able to compete equally for a higher education. My ancestor's education seems primitive compared to my own.

"The schools I have attended in my sixteen years have never lacked the ability necessary for me to achieve a higher education, nor has my social position kept me from doing so.

"I now attend one of the best high schools in the United States and my education has gone twice as far as my parents and three times as far as their parents. The knowledge and experience

I have gained over these years of education have placed me in a position to succeed, unlike my forefathers who were restricted because of external forces."

TRIBUTE FROM THE LATE SEN. RUSSELL B. LONG
ON THE OCCASION OF THE FUNERAL OF GUY B. JACKSON

(In another part of Rattlesnake Mountain was the vacation residence of the late US Senator Russell B. Long (D-LA). Senator Long gave me permission to reprint his remarks at the funeral of Guy B. Jackson.)

"If everybody could have been like Guy Jackson, there would have been no wars. The sheriff would have needed no deputies. He would have had less to do than the Maytag Repair Man. The Chief of Police would have spent his time directing travelers to their destination. Our jails would have had no locks on the doors. They would have been emergency shelters for persons in dire distress.

"Long before I met Guy Jackson, I had been told he was a perfect gentleman in every sense of the word.

"So, one night when I found my car stuck on the narrow roads of Rattlesnake Mountain, I headed for his home. His response was instant. There was no question of _whether_ he should come out into the damp night to help a stranger. His thought turned instantly to how he could help best.

"After he pulled my car out of the mud he asked for nothing. Typical of Guy Jackson, he seldom asked for anything for helping those who sought him, and he never complained if they paid him nothing after he had gone to a lot of trouble to help them.

"No doubt a lot of less worthy people took advantage of Guy Jackson's helpful, generous, neighborly ways, but to people of substance, he was like a precious jewel to be treasured and admired.

"God knows how dependable Guy Jackson was. So did all his neighbors and friends from highway 55 to Rattlesnake Mountain top. It was that way whether you came by way of Belle Meade or Kinden.

"The power company had a rural line reaching Rattlesnake Mountain. In bad weather it was usually the first out and the last back in service. The power company had standing instructions for their power crews:

'If you need help in the area near Africa School House, call on Guy Jackson.'

"Many times, I have passed Guy Jackson's home on a Sunday afternoon to witness what appeared to be an overcrowded parking lot. His daughters, their husbands and children would frequently use the afternoon of the Sabbath to make the young people know their Grandpa. What an inspiration he must have been for all of them!

"He was an inspiration for me, for my wife Carolyn, and for my neighbors the Jessups.

"God has a way of granting a long life to those who he chooses for special duty. He did so with Moses and Noah.

"But their life is only the beginning when they leave us on this planet. God has plans for such willing workers in his Kingdom of the hereafter.

We are fortunate to have Guy for so many years. Now he is with God.

"Let me express my love to Marsha, his daughters, grandchildren and relatives.

"If we are worthy of Guy Jackson's love, we will see him again in a setting of joy."

- Russell B. Long

Harlan Westover and his wife Esta were pioneer Blue Mountaineers
and were neighbors of author Dick Long.

- 20 -
THE WESTOVERS -
ENDING UP WHERE IT ALL BEGAN

The Spring of 1971 was a most exciting time for me at Blue Mountain. It was the time my house went up. I even took off from work in Washington just to go out and see it rise on the mountain. And it began to look the way I wanted it to look: like one of those large mountain chalets I had admired in my early years in the Adirondacks.

One of my sometime visitors when the house was being built was a wondrous, six-year-old boy by the name of Alexander. And he didn't go by "Al" or "Alex". No. When he first came to watch he introduced himself as: "I'm Alexander Westover. I'm your neighbor. I live down there," as he pointed toward a clump of trees.

Houses, I was to learn, are rarely visible at Blue Mountain, even tho they are only a few hundred feet apart. This is due to the genius of the founder, Henry de Longfief. Each house at Blue Mountain, in the beginning, had to be built seventy feet from the road. Also, only a minimum of trees were to be removed to make way for a house and a road. Thus there was the feelings that each house was its own mountain kingdom, isolated from the rest.

So, when Alexander pointed to where he lived all I saw was a stand of trees, even tho the Westovers were my next door neighbors.

Having my house built at Blue Mountain precipitated my first fearful encounter with Henry de Longfief. In 1971 there were very few houses that had not been built by Blue Mountain Construction Co., Henry and Colette's company. If you wanted to build your own house the plans had to be approved by Henry. The horror stories when people took this route were legend. Some of the plans were rejected. Some people got so mad they sold their lots and never returned to Blue Mountain.

Also, in 1971 Henry was only building one or two types or houses. They were nice models but I preferred a larger house. I had a discussion with Henry and his estimate for the shell of the type of house I wanted was too costly. I could only afford a shell, at this time. I decided to pursue other avenues, other builders. When I told other Blue Mountaineers about this they cautioned: "You better not...It is not a good idea. You better let Henry build it."

But, I had become very attracted to one model, The Mont Blanc, built by Northern Counties Lumber of Upperville, Virginia. This model, with a natural wood siding and an 18-foot cathedral ceiling, reminded me of some of the rugged, natural- looking mountain homes or "camps" I had seen in the Adirondack Mountains. Also, the shell of that model, even enlarged more, as I wanted it, with a screen porch, was less than the price Henry quoted.

I wrote to Henry telling him that I decided to have Northern Counties build my house. He wrote back, tersely: "Please submit the plans. Nothing will be built until I approve it."

Fearfully I submitted the plans. The response came back quickly. Surprisingly Henry approved the plan. He liked the model, except for some minor changes.

I remember telling Bill Leachman, the president of Northern Counties, that Henry OK'd the house plans.

Leachman, who later died in a plane crash, was incredulous.

"Are you kidding," he said. "You mean he approved it. Well, I'll be. That's the first one of ours he ever approved. We've never built up there before. He wouldn't allow it. You must have a magic wand."

After my house had been up for a year I had an interesting comment from one of my neighbors who was a year-round resident.

"This may or may not surprise you," he said, "but a lot of people stop to admire your house. And some of these people are prospective lot and house buyers who are with Henry or Colette."

Shortly afterwards Blue Mountain came out with a new model they called "Shenendoah". The house was similar to mine, only smaller. The "Shenandoah" has been one of the more popular Blue Mountain models for the past 18 years.

As the weeks and months went by I gradually met my neighbors. I say gradually because Blue Mountain is a "gradual" place. It is like people were saying: the trees and the rocks have been here for a long time, so let us take some time to get to know each other. Blue Mountain is not an instantly social place. People like to enjoy their own spaces in a quiet manner; take walks in the forest; admire all the beauties of nature.

One of my extrovertive friends from Washington came to visit me once, only once.

"How do you stand it up here, it is so quiet?, he said. "This sure ain't Ocean City!"

I muttered something like "Thank God, it isn't."

Blue Mountain isn't for everyone. The beach, I agreed with my friend, is quite an exciting place, in many ways. But at that time in my life I had a very exciting, high pressure job in Washington. By the time Friday rolled around I didn't need any more excitement. I was ready for some peace and quiet. And that usually took the shape of a weekend with a few friends. As soon as we got onto 66 west (which in those days was only completed to Gainesville) we all felt immense relief. And we usually broke into a hearty rendition of John Denver's "Country Roads."

Eventually, through six-year-old Alexander, I got to meet the rest of the Westover family. There were a family of six: Harlan and Esta Westover, the parents; Marcus was the oldest son and two daughters: Martina and Victoria. It was very warm outgoing family and for this bachelor (I was in my forties then) I felt like I became part of their lives on Blue Mountain. And whenever members of my family came down from Syracuse or new visitors to Blue Mountain I always felt comfortable introducing them to the Westovers.

We had some things in common: a love for Blue Mountain; we were Washington types who had had our share of world travels and, we felt like pioneers in the forest, as there were not that many people on the mountain yet. They had come to Blue Mountain in 1968, two years before my arrival in 1970.

The Westovers were different in one distinctive way. Because Esta was a native-born Austrian I always had a feeling of being in a European home. I came to learn that this was true of several Blue Mountain households. Many couples or families where one partner was American and the other was European-American had bought property and had homes on Blue Mountain.

I think this happened because of the de Longfief's French-American background. It was another example of Henry's diversified life that he would attract people from many different backgrounds. I also learned that Europeans, probably because they do not have as much forest land as Americans, treasure their forest more than we do.

"The first time I saw where we were going to build," Esta recalled, "I exclaimed: 'the Weiner Wald, the Weiner Wald", referring to the Vienna Woods that she loved so much as a child.

"Any time any Europeans, or especially Austrians, would come to Blue Mountain they would feel the same way. It was amazing," she said.

I always felt that the Westovers were a very close and loving couple. And this was reflected in many ways, especially in the great care and devotion they had for their children. I used to like to hear Harlan and Esta recall how they met and fell in love in Vienna.

It was in the Korean war days of the 1950s. Harlan was with the Army Security Agency in Washington. He was assigned to Vienna and was in charge of detachment of American troops. Vienna, during those days was occupied by the major powers. It was a focal point in the Cold War.

"Harlan spoke fluent Russian," Esta said. Some Russians said they couldn't tell whether it was a Russian speaking or an American."

During the time Harlan was in Vienna the coronation of Queen Elizabeth II was taking place in London.

"A friend of mine and myself had been invited to the British Embassy for a reception," Harlan said. "We had a difficult time finding it. We asked a young lady how to get there. The lady was Esta. Well, one thing led to another....."Harlan recalled.

"I picked him up," Esta laughs.

During most of their time in Washington the Westovers lived on Capitol Hill, in 1966 they spent the summer on a farm near Luray in the Shenandoah Valley. "A lady doctor, a microbiologist, who taught medicine at George Washington University Hospital, had a heart surgeon friend, who owned an old house and she let us take that place for a month," Esta said. "We really enjoyed it. Harlan did his first paintings there. I think it was the first time we thought seriously about getting a place in the country."

Harlan, at the time, was working at the Department f Commerce. During the next year he was also doing some volunteer work at an agency that helped the poor. One of the people at the agency, Henry Trepanter, had a place at Blue Mountain on Trilium trail.

Harlan had expressed fears that things "were beginning to boil over in Washington", a fear that came true the next summer, 1968, when the riots occurred. It would be good to get the kids out of the city for the summer, Harlan thought.

"Henry said he had a friend at Blue Mountain who was going to England for the summer and would not be using his cabin. He said he would be glad to have someone in it. So we rented it. That's how we came to Blue Mountain for the first time."

"We drove around the mountain that summer thinking about buying land," Esta said.

"Did you know Henry at that time," I asked Esta.

"Oh," said Esta exuberantly, "Henry de Longfief was the first person I met. We moved in one night and the next morning there was Henry at the door.

"He said 'hello, I am Henry de Longfief. I must tell you I have to know who is here.' That's what he said."

Esta said that Henry came to visit them every day.

"I didn't drive and we didn't have a dog. I appreciated his concern. He made us feel safe up here. I appreciated this right away," Esta said. "I learned this later," Esta said, "that Henry would make visits to all of the houses on a regular basis. He kept people in line. And they had this feeling this Blue Mountain would stay the way he started it. He was on top of everything. And you felt secure.

"When something happened Henry would be right there. Many times the children had injuries. Henry would come and make sure they got to the doctor.

He was always available for everything."

Esta told Henry one day: "Maybe it is a dream, but we would like to have a little place someday, on the mountain."

They took a ride around the mountain, looking at various locations.

"Give me the darkest place, with a lot of trees, where it is really cool, I told Henry," and then with a laugh she said, "lots of light."

"I gave Henry this impossible request. Well, he showed us this place. It was lot three-thirty-three. So that is my number. So this was it. That is how it started," she said.

"That was in 1967. Harlan and I discussed it more. We called Henry in January and said 'start building as soon as you can.' He started in March, 1968 and we moved in on June 2, 1968, our wedding anniversary."

Like me, the Westovers started with a shell and filled it in as the months and years passed.

Their oldest son, Marcus, was in Europe in 1967 so he missed the family's first experience at Blue Mountain on Trilium Trail.

"Marcus was so excited when he came up here. The front porch was still open so Harlan put a rope around. I said 'that won't keep them from falling off.' Sure enough I heard this thud. Alexander fell off the porch. It was quite a drop. Alexander said 'I fell.' Harlan said 'he landed on his bottom. He's OK.' And Alexander would find snakes. He would come and say 'Mama, there's a copperhead down there.' I would say: 'No Alex, you are teasing.' So, I would go down to look and sure enough there was a copperhead hissing at me.' So that's how we started at Blue Mountain with people falling of the front porch and Alexander finding snakes. But, it has been fun."

Harlan, at this writing (1991) has retired from his government job. He and Esta decided to live year-round at Blue Mountain. Harlan suffers from a heart condition but is able to get about, just not as quickly as the old days.

"We were snowed in three times last winter," Harlan said. But, you know, this place has a beauty in the wintertime that is special. We didn't mind. On a June day in 1991 I visited the Westovers with Donald Mankin, my photographer friend.

I was pleasantly surprised. Their place is not what can be called "finished" and is it beautiful.

The grounds are tastefully landscaped. There is a quiet beauty there. None of the elegant, tall trees have been removed. But clearing has been made around them, giving a feeling of depth and beauty in the forest. The Westover home, more than most homes at Blue Mountain, fits perfectly and naturally with the forest around it.

Visiting the Westovers, for me, was like completing the cycle of more than twenty years It was going back to my Blue Mountain roots.

We talked about the people we all knew in the beginning: Agnes McDonald, the Singletons, Lee Lipscomb, the Machados, the Hiles and the McReights. Several had moved away, sold their places. But several had stayed, too, giving Blue Mountain its historic continuity. I had sold my house to my brother Bob and then he sold it in 1987. But, I still own a lot, down the road, not far from the Westovers.

"You'll build again, you'll come back," Esta laughed.

I assured Esta and Harlan I would certainly like to, if conditions, in the future, permit.

Looking out at the green beauty in front of us I said: "I miss Alexander's tree house."

The first time I met Alexander in 1971, at his home (after several inspection trips to my house under construction) he was sitting in a tree house in front of the main house.

This remembrance brought up talk of "The Poison Ivy Theatre."

"It was our own Blue Mountain theatre," Harlan said. Vicky and Martina wrote the plays and then all of the children acted in them.

The tree house was for the balcony scenes. Alexander played a lady bug, once. That was one of his major roles.

I was interested in what happened to their four children.

Marcus, I was impressed to hear, has been District of Columbia police officer for several years. He is now a lieutenant and works in Anacostia, one of the most difficult assignments on the force.

"He always wanted a challenge and I think he had found it. Although I do get worried," Esta said.

Martina went to Europe for her studies and met her future husband, Raphael Monzies, there. Martina is a painter and Raphael is a teacher and he also builds houses. They live in Saint Laurent, France.

Victoria, who lives in Baltimore, has had a career as a writer and photographer and is in charge of a Baltimore Film Festival. She is married to a professional artist Michael Bailey. Alexander who is on the DMZ, Korea is considering a career with the US Army.

They all come back to their Blue Mountain home, from time to time. And now that additions have been made there is room for all.

After a wonderful lunch, prepared by Esta, it was time for us to take our leave.

As Donald and I walked the path from their house, I suddenly remembered something I wanted to say.

"You know," I said, as we walked away, and I looked back at their house nestled in the forest, "I think Henry would really like how your place turned out. It is just beautiful."

"Yes," Esta said, as she smiled and waved back to us. "Yes, I think he would."

EPILOGUE

As I have stated previously, Blue Mountain Memories, was researched and written over a period of several years. I was interrupted in this process several times. My various journalism jobs kept me busy and I had a long stretch as a documentary filmmaker for the Federal Government.

But I always came back to the research and writing. It was like Blue Mountain was a long lost love, that I always wanted to keep experiencing. The people of Blue Mountain were so interesting and the serendipity of how we all found this wilderness only 65 miles from the Nation's Capital, has never stopped being intriguing.

There was also, through the years, the discouragement that many writers face. I could not find a publisher for the book—either in the Virginia Blue Ridge communities, Washington, DC or in my native Upstate New York.

The manuscript got dusty and worn as it sat in various basements for the past ten to fifteen years. Last year a light appeared at the end of the tunnel. I got a call from Blue Mountain resident Jack Davis. He had organized a committee at Blue Mountain to look into its history.

He had heard about my research and that I may have a manuscript about Blue Mountain. He said that his group would be glad to assist me in trying to find a publisher. It was certainly encouraging to me. It brought new life into these old bones.

The committee did not have any luck in finding a publisher. I appreciated their efforts. I extended my search again but, over the year. I was unsuccessful too. But all's well that end well. A close friend made a profit on a business deal. I can still hear her voice on the phone: "Let's get your book published." And thanks to her that is how Blue Mountain Memories finally became this book.

There has been tremendous joy working on this project. Truly a labor of love. But there is also some sadness. Because the project took so long to come to fruition, there have been several deaths over the years.

I couldn't finish the book without mentioning the following Blue Mountaineers, especially those who are the subjects of the various chapters. Several deaths are mentioned in this the book, like de Longfiefs, Charlie Reynolds and others.

However, it saddened me to learn of the following more recent deaths:

Polly Frederick, Lee Lipscomb, Agnes McDonald, Harrell Clark.

Anne Anderson, Eric and Helga Heiberg related a touching story…Helga suggested, after Polly Frederick's death, that the small bridge over a creek going into Deer Lake be named after her. It was named: Pont du Polly.

I know that I will not have all of them mentioned as we go to press. However I am sure that others will be mentioned in the regular Blue Mountain publication.

BIBLIOGRAPHY FOR "BLUE MOUNTAIN MEMORIES"

The Battle of Cedar Creek, Joseph A. Whitehorne

Fall Leaves, the Civil War Letters of Major Henry Livermore Abbott, Kent State University Press.

Four Valiant Years, Laura Virginia Hale, Shenandoah Publishing House

The Foxes Union, James J. Kilpatrick, EPM Publications, Inc

Frederick County, Virginia, From the Frontier to the Future, Rebecca A. Ebert and Teresa Lazazzera, The Donning Co. Publishers, Norfolk/Virginia Beach, VA

The Guns of Cedar Creek, Thomas A. Lewis, Harper and Row, New York

High in Old Virginia's Piedmont, A History of Marshall, Faquier County, John K. Gott, Marshall National Bank and Trust Co., Marshall, VA

Journals of Amanda Virginia Edmonds: Lass of the Mosby Confederacy, 1859-1867, Edited by Nancy Chappelear Baird

Jubal Early's Raid on Washington, 1864, B.F. Cooling, the Nautical and Aviation Publishing Co. of America, Inc., Baltimore, MD

The Marble Man, Robert E. Lee and His Image in American Society, Thomas Connelly, Alfred Knopf, New York

Men and Events of the Revloution in Winchester and Frederick County, Virginia, Winchester-Frederick County Historical Society Papers

Ranger Mosby, Virgil Carrington Jones, EPM Publications, McLean, VA, Reprint, Originally published University of North Carolina Press, Chapel Hill, NC

Ruggles Regiment, the 122nd NY Volunteers in the American Civil War, David Swinfen, University Press of New England

Sad Earth, Sweet Heaven The Story of Front Royal in the Civil War, by Lucy Buck

Shenandoah, The Valley Story, by Alvin Dohme, Greatland Publishing Co., Front Royal, VA

Virginia Baron, The Story of Thomas 6th Lord Fairfax, Stuart E. Brown, Chesapeake Book Company, Berryville, VA